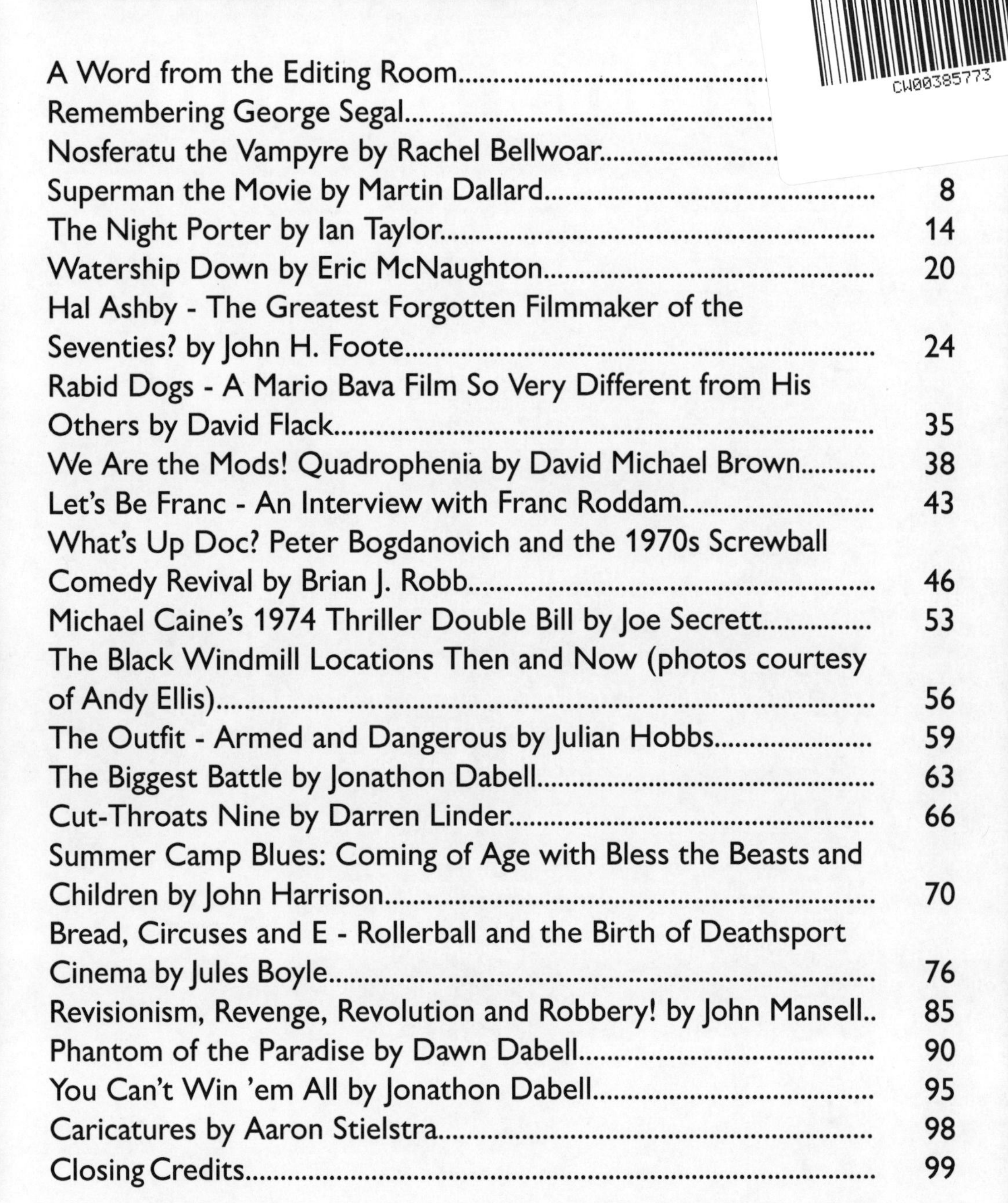

OPENING CREDITS

Contributors this issue: Rachel Bellwoar, Jules Boyle, David Michael Brown, Dawn Dabell, Jonathon Dabell, Martin Dallard, Andy Ellis, David Flack, John H. Foote, John Harrison, Julian Hobbs, Darren Linder, Eric McNaughton, John Mansell, Brian J. Robb, Joe Secrett, Ian Taylor. Caricature artwork by Aaron Stielstra. Phantom of the Paradise additional artwork by Paul Garner (www.etsy.com/uk/shop/PaulGarnerMonsterArt)

Design and Layout: Dawn Dabell
Copy Editor: Jonathon Dabell

Printed globally by Amazon KDP

A Word from the Editing Room

Greetings! Issue 3 of 'Cinema of the '70s' is in your hands, and we're confident you'll enjoy our latest fabulous assortment of reviews, overviews and interviews. This time, for your reading pleasure, we're delighted to offer an eclectic mix of material looking at everything from Hollywood blockbusters like *Superman the Movie* to obscure Euro westerns like *Cut-Throats Nine*.

May we begin by introducing several new writers from our ever-expanding pool. A warm welcome to Martin Dallard, who covers Richard Donner's *Superman* (1978); Julian Hobbs, who casts his eye over the hard-hitting crime thriller *The Outfit* (1973); and Rachel Bellwoar, who takes a look at Werner Herzog's atmospheric *Nosferatu the Vampyre* (1979).

Our cover article by John H. Foote is an examination of the '70s films of director Hal Ashby. John covers the director's run of seven consecutive classics from the decade, discussing how and why he was relatively forgotten alongside contemporary big hitters likes Steven Spielberg, Francis Ford Coppola, George Lucas and Brian de Palma.

We also have articles about fare as diverse as *The Night Porter* (1974), *Bless the Beasts and Children* (1971), *Watership Down* (1978), *Phantom of the Paradise* (1974), and much more. We also have a never-before-published interview with Franc Roddam, the director of cult favourite *Quadrophenia* (1979), as well as an accompanying article on the film itself.

We continue to be excited and surprised by the creative process of putting this magazine together. We never cease to be amazed by our writers' passion, their research, knowledge and enthusiasm. Their articles contain many nuggets of information as well as insightful observations and opinions. As we have said in previous issues, it is a pleasure to put these publications together - we trust our readers will experience the same mix of enjoyment and education when leafing through the mag.

So, until the next time, goodbye… and happy reading!

Dawn and Jonathon Dabell

Remembering George Segal (1934-2021)

In March 2021, George Segal died due to complications related to heart bypass surgery. He was 87. Segal rose to prominence in the '60s in films like *King Rat* (1965), *Who's Afraid of Virginia Woolf?* and *The Quiller Memorandum* (both 1966). He received a Best Supporting Actor Oscar nomination for his work on *Virginia Woolf*, losing out to Walter Matthau in *The Fortune Cookie*. In the '70s, he cemented his status as a leading man, enjoying a fine run of memorable films. Segal remained active until his death, most recently appearing in the long-running TV show *The Goldbergs* as Albert 'Pops' Solomon.

His '70s films were:
Loving (1970)
Where's Poppa? (1970)
The Owl and the Pussycat (1970)
Born to Win (1971)
The Hot Rock (1972)
Blume in Love (1972)
A Touch of Class (1973)
The Terminal Man (1974)
California Split (1974)
Russian Roulette (1975)
The Black Bird (1975)
The Duchess and the Dirtwater Fox (1976)
Fun with Dick and Jane (1977)
Rollercoaster (1977)
Who Is Killing the Great Chefs of Europe? (1978)
Lost and Found (1979)

Farewell, Mr. Segal… and thanks for the memories.

In Memoriam

Ned Beatty
(1937-2021)
Actor, known for *Deliverance* (1972), *All the President's Men* (1976) and *Network* (1976).

Shane Briant
(1946-2021)
Actor known for *Straight on Till Morning* (1972) and *Captain Kronos, Vampire Hunter* (1974).

Charles Grodin
(1935-2021)
Actor, known for *The Heartbreak Kid* (1972), *King Kong (1976) and Heaven Can Wait* (1978).

James Hampton
(1936-2021)
Actor, known for *Hawmps!* (1976) and *The China Syndrome* (1979).

Monte Hellman
(1929-2021)
Director, known for *Two-Lane Blacktop* (1971) and *Cockfighter* (1974).

Yaphet Kotto
(1939-2021)
Actor, known for *Across 110th Street* (1972), *Blue Collar* (1978) and *Alien* (1979).

Richard Rush
(1929-2021)
Director, known for *Getting Straight* (1970) and *Freebie and the Bean* (1974).

Isela Vega
(1939-2021)
Actress, known for *Bring Me the Head of Alfredo Garcia* (1974) and *Drum* (1976).

Jessica Walter
(1941-2021)
Actress, known for *Play Misty For Me* (1971) and *Victory at Entebbe* (1976).

Norman J. Warren
(1935-2021)
Director, known for *Satan's Slave* (1976) and *Prey* (1977).

Nosferatu the Vampyre

by Rachel Bellwoar

Following *Aguirre, the Wrath of God* (1972), *Nosferatu the Vampyre* (1979) marked the second collaboration of Klaus Kinski and director Werner Herzog. Kinski wasn't the easiest actor to work with and, after his death in 1991, Herzog directed a documentary about their relationship entitled *My Best Fiend* (1999).

Regardless of what went on behind the scenes, their films together are masterworks. In the case of *Nosferatu the Vampyre*, that's all the more remarkable given the high esteem in which F. W. Murnau's original *Nosferatu* (1922) is held, both as a silent film and a horror classic. Watching them together, there's no question that certain scenes owe a lot to Murnau, and that's intentional. But Herzog puts his own mark on the story, and he could never be accused of aping Murnau's *Nosferatu* nor Bram Stoker's *Dracula*. Rather, he delivers his own essential vampire movie.

At the center of all three of these stories is the relationship between Jonathan Harker and his wife, Mina. In a vain attempt to avoid being sued for copyright infringement, many of the characters go by different names in Murnau's *Nosferatu* (though for this essay I'm going to use Stoker's names), and in Herzog's version Mina goes by the name Lucy (which, confusingly, is the name of Mina's friend in *Dracula*). The first time we meet the happy couple in Murnau's *Nosferatu*, it's like they're in a different movie. Jonathan (Gustav von Wangenheim) is picking flowers while Mina (Greta Schröder) is playing with some kittens. Herzog's Mina, or Lucy (Isabelle Adjani), is introduced waking up from a nightmare. Technically this is before Dracula's name has even been mentioned, yet Herzog takes advantage of the fact that viewers will be familiar with the story and doesn't waste any time explaining her dream. Instead of Murnau's fake out, Herzog gets straight to the point and there's never any doubt that you're watching a horror movie.

Harker's call to adventure comes when he's told Count Dracula wants to buy a house in Wismar. In *Dracula* it's London, and in Murnau's *Nosferatu* the property being purchased is in Germany, but in every case the important bit is that Harker must travel to Transylvania to finalise the sale.

In Stoker's 'Dracula', Harker's boss is named Mr. Hawkins, while Dracula's servant Renfield is a separate character. In both *Nosferatu* films, the characters are combined so Renfield fulfills Mr. Hawkins' purpose of sending Harker to Transylvania. He's an otherwise forgettable character anyway, so omitting him isn't a bad move, but it does raise the question of how Renfield ever got hired as an estate agent, moreover in a position of authority! His most

istinctive trait in Herzog's version is his laugh. According o Herzog's commentary on the Shout! Factory Blu-Ray elease, it was after hearing Roland Topor's laugh that he new Topor was ideal for the role (though, in both the nglish and German versions, his voice is dubbed).

How Harker (Bruno Ganz) gets to Transylvania in Herzog's *Nosferatu* is notably different from how he gets here in Murnau's film and Stoker's novel. Namely, he nakes the journey on horseback instead of taking public ransportation. Dracula's castle is remote, which is one of he reasons the trip is so dangerous. But in Herzog's film, Harker spends most of the trip alone - to the point that t's unclear why Herzog even bothers to have the carriage ick him up for the final stretch. Since Herzog opts out f having the carriage driver be Count Dracula in disguise, t would've made more sense if Harker completed the ourney on his own.

If Herzog doesn't get across how long the journey took Harker tells Count Dracula four weeks but in the film it eels like days), he does make it clear how arduous it was, ısing real locations like he did in *Aguirre, the Wrath of God* o create a sense of scale and awe around nature.

Harker's isolation (which is paralleled by his wife Lucy's n the latter half of the movie) is central to Herzog's *Nosferatu* because it gives the film its cynical edge. In Stoker's 'Dracula', the whole reason Dracula is defeated s because Harker teams up with Dr. Van Helsing and his als. Their camaraderie is supposed to be their biggest dvantage. But in Herzog's *Nosferatu*, Lucy and Jonathan re just as isolated as Dracula, especially after Dracula rings the plague to Wismar. It's like a German *The Bed Sitting Room* (1969), with every man for himself and people clinging to appearances.

In Herzog's English commentary for the Shout! Factory Blu-Ray, he describes Kinski's Dracula as being human. Today Max Schreck's performance in Murnau's original is iconic, but his Dracula is much more tied to he supernatural. Schreck's Dracula doesn't open doors. They open for him or he walks through them. Kinski's Dracula is much more grounded in reality. He's a monster out a monster whose nocturnal lifestyle has left him with shadows under his eyes. An outsider - hunched over and pathetic - it's that contrast which makes him scary because t breeds doubt. Someone so awkward, pouring wine with ong fingernails, shouldn't be able to use eye contact like a weapon but Kinski's Dracula does, and it's his ability to turn the violence on and off which makes him terrifying in what's an extremely physical performance.

Upon meeting for the first time, Harker lets Dracula do most of the talking, but there's still a lot of silence. Indeed, a lot of the choreography throughout feels like it's out of a silent movie (which Murnau's *Nosferatu* was), and it's nteresting to see those aspects maintained in Herzog's version. The hand motions are exaggerated. Adjani's hair

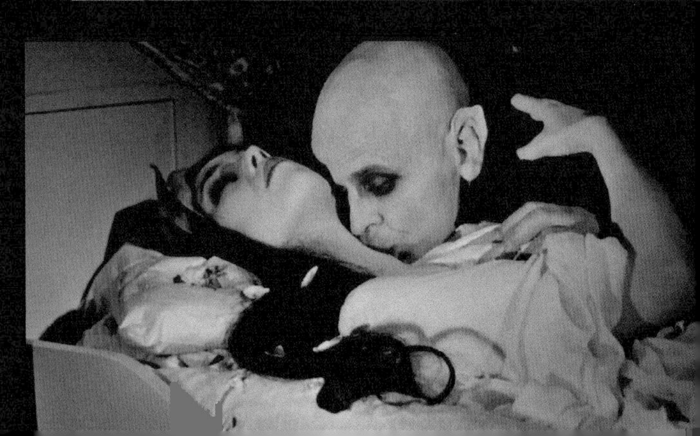

looks like it's alive in the scene where she meets Dracula in person.

In Stoker's 'Dracula' there weren't any mirrors in Dracula's castle. Vampires don't have reflections, so this makes sense. But it also means it's never clear if Dracula has sucked Harker's blood, because there's no moment where he sees the bite marks in a mirror. One of the best scenes in Herzog's version is the one where Dracula meets Lucy because Herzog does utilize mirrors. Instead of being faithful to the novel, Dracula gets an amazing entrance.

As for Dr. Van Helsing (Walter Ladengast), in Stoker's 'Dracula' all of the characters defer to him and it's easy to get swept up in the hero worship, but nobody ever calls him out for withholding information. Had he not insisted on keeping his friends in the dark, it's possible certain mistakes could've been avoided. By using his own words (or at least a similar corn metaphor to the one he makes in Stoker's novel) against him, Herzog is able to show Van Helsing as being flawed in a way that would've never been entertained by the characters in the novel.

Reading 'Dracula' and watching Murnau's *Nosferatu*, there's never any doubt that Jonathan and Mina love each other. Granted, Jonathan has some patriarchal views about what marriage should be but that doesn't make his love any less sincere. If anything, Herzog makes their love story even more integral to the plot of *Nosferatu*, whether it's Jonathan finding the drive to escape Dracula's castle when he realizes Lucy's in danger or fighting off the effects of getting bitten (which didn't seem to faze Wangenheim's Jonathan at all in the silent version). While Mina's actions are heroic in Murnau's *Nosferatu*, it's always with the caveat that women are the weaker sex. In Herzog's *Nosferatu*, Lucy gets to have more agency. She doesn't read Jonathan's 'Book of the Vampires' because she can't resist the temptation. She does it to stay informed. And it's in recognition of how much Lucy loves Jonathan that Dracula thinks he can blackmail her.

Later Kinski would star in a sequel to *Nosferatu the Vampyre* called *Vampire in Venice* (1988). Herzog wasn't involved in the project and, in the documentary *Creation is Violent: Anecdotes from Kinski's Final Years* (2021), some fuss is made over Kinski refusing to wear the makeup that he wore in Herzog's movie or a bald cap. That the film disregards vampire rules isn't mentioned, nor the fact that a true sequel ought to have followed the character of Jonathan. You can't blame the production company for wanting to capture lightning in a bottle twice - it's just that it can't always be done that way.

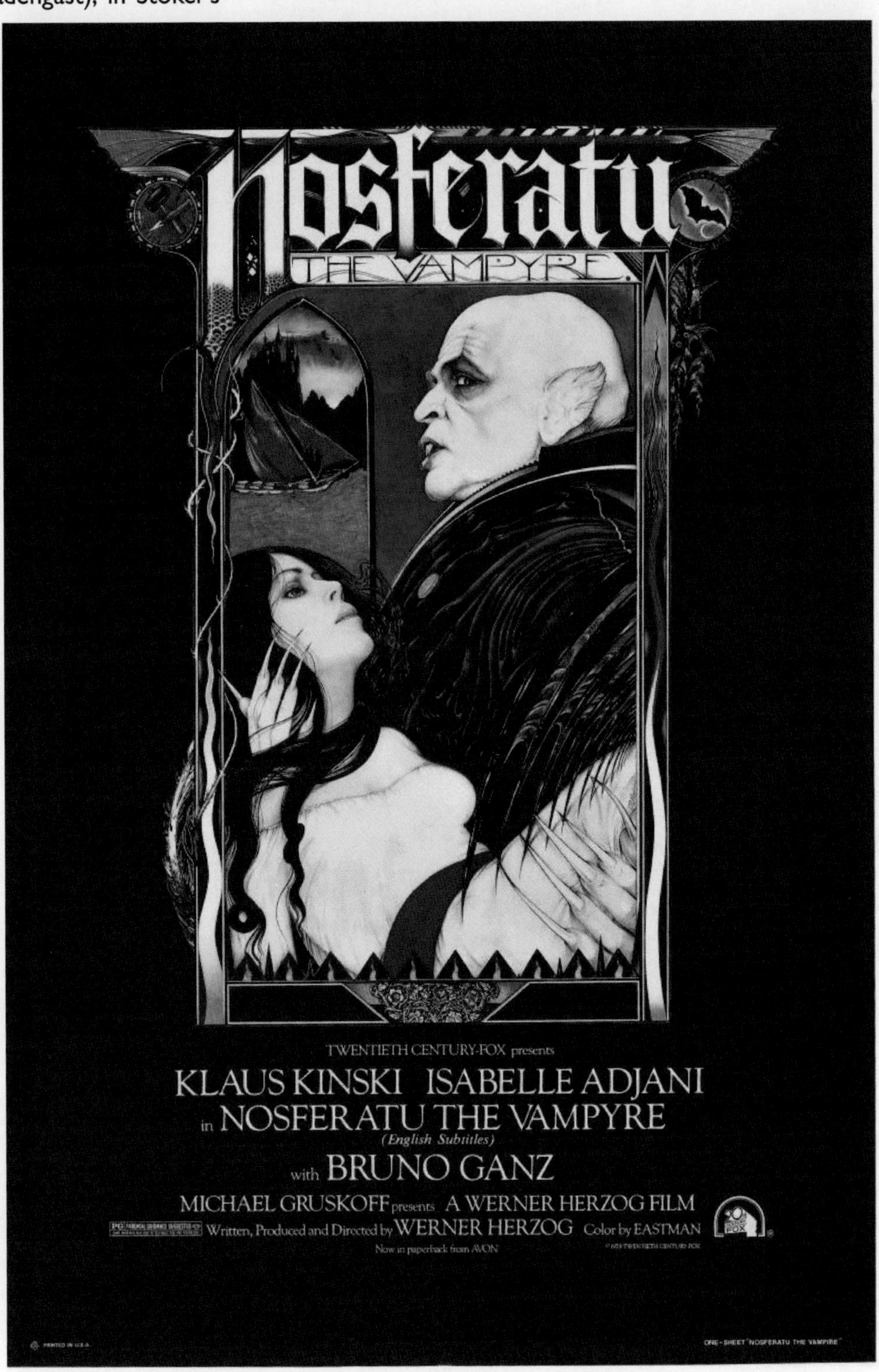

SUPERMAN THE MOVIE

by Martin Dallard

The tentpole superhero movie that set the standard, and has never been bettered!

Superman the Movie blasted its way onto cinema screens around the world in the winter of 1978. It took a whole four years to get there, with many a tear shed along the way.

In 1974, flushed with the success of *The Three Musketeers*, producers Alexander and Ilya Salkind and their partner Pierre Spengler were hunting for the next big thing to bring to cinema screens. They finally settled on *Superman*. No-one was really interested in the superhero genre at this point. Perhaps the memory of the campy Adam West *Batman* television show was still fresh in their minds.

It took the visionary talent of the Salkinds to see that the time was right for a *Superman* movie. Warner Bros owned D.C. Comics, which in turn produced the numerous 'Superman' comic books on a monthly basis. Even *they* couldn't see the potential of such a project. They simply didn't possess the foresight to consider translating the Last Son of Krypton to the silver screen.

In order to get the idea across to Warners, the Salkinds needed some leverage, something which would make the giant studio sit up and pay attention. They needed to get big names involved, and who better to start with than writer Mario Puzo of *The Godfather* fame? He was brought in to handle the writing duties after William Goldman had turned them down. Once Puzo had agreed to pen the script, the Salkinds had more credibility and could start trying to attract bankable actors to the project.

The final stamp of approval came when iconic actor Marlon Brando signed on to play Superman's Kryptonian father, Jor El. Brando was paid a whopping $3.7 million for two weeks work, making him the highest paid actor in Hollywood up to that point. Hot on Brando's heels, Gene Hackman was asked to play Superman's arch-nemesis Lex Luthor. When first approached, Hackman was reluctant to take the role, thinking such a cartoon villain would tarnish his credibility as a serious actor. It took a while before he realised he could bring real depth to this seemingly two-dimensional character.

The combined talents of Puzo, Brando and Hackman gave the production the required gravitas. Now they could look to attract financing from multi-national sources to get *Superman* 'off the ground', so to speak.

The Salkinds next needed a director to steer the ship, and they needed someone with vision equal to their own. They initially settled on British director Guy Hamilton, famous for his James Bond epics, since he obviously had a flair for drama as well as major action sequences. At the same time, they brought additional writers Robert Benton and David & Leslie Newman aboard to take another swing at Puzo's massive script, tightening and rewriting where required.

While all this was taking shape, preproduction began in Italy where the majority of the film was to be shot. But at the eleventh hour everything changed, as it became more viable from a financial perspective to do the filming in England where the Salkinds would get more bangs for their bucks. This brought with it an unwanted headache, as director Hamilton was a tax exile from the U.K. and could only spend thirty days a year on British soil. There was no way he could oversee such a massive production in such a short space of time so, reluctantly, Hamilton bowed out… leaving the director's seat vacant.

But not for long.

Due to 1976's *The Omen,* and the phenomenal box office receipts it had garnered, the directing baton was offered to Richard Donner. Legend has it that the deal was struck with Donner on a Sunday morning whilst the director was sitting on toilet minding his own business!

Donner was offered a million dollars to shoot two *Superman* films back-to-back. The Salkinds had come up with this approach when filming the *Musketeers* movie and its sequel simultaneously. Donner agreed, and it was the sheer fact that the director was now on board that got Hackman to cement his commitment to the Luthor role. Up to that point, he had still been on the fence regarding the project.

One of Donner's first tasks was to bring in screenwriter Tom Mankiewicz to help refine the script. The director's ideas were radically different to those of the producers. As the script stood, it was a sort of parody of a parody, and Donner considered this worse than sacrilege. It almost felt like it dishonoured the American flag and everything Superman stood for.

In order to make the film "fly," it needed a healthy dose of verisimilitude. With this in mind, Mankiewicz's rewrite focussed mainly on the characterisation, especially the relationships of Superman and Lois, and Lois and Clark. He honed the script, making sure viewers cared more about the core characters.

Talking of Superman and Lois Lane, these two vital roles were yet to be cast. Donner wanted an unknown for Clark Kent, not the likes of Paul Newman or Robert Redford who would cast a shadow even larger than the iconic character. Against Donner's wishes, many leading men in Hollywood - from Dustin Hoffman to Clint Eastwood - were offered the title role, though none was willing to risk donning the famous red and blue tights.

Relative newcomer Nick Nolte was offered the part, but by this point Donner had already auditioned a relative unknown by the name of Christopher Reeve, and, even though the young man was a six-foot-four string bean, Donner liked him. He believed he'd found the ideal candidate in Reeve to play the dual roles of Kal El and Clark.

Reeve practically lied his way into the audition, saying that he used to be a high school jock and had lost a lot of weight since taking up acting. He promised he would have no trouble putting it all back on. He even wore the biggest sweater he could find to bulk up his frame at the audition. Regardless, Donner saw his potential, and it helped that Reeve certainly looked like his comic book counterpart.

By hook or by crook, Donner convinced the Salkinds to go with the unknown Reeve. The director told the young actor he was taking a huge risk entrusting him with such a plum part. Reeve committed himself one hundred percent, training with Dave Prowse (who had played Darth Vader in *Star Wars*) and packing on over thirty pounds of muscle during pre-production.

All that was left was to find Lois Lane, and the casting directors cast a wide net. Once again, they screen-tested the royalty of Hollywood, before settling on Canadian actress Margot Kidder who they thought showed a great screen chemistry with Reeve. (Reeve helped many of the actresses during their auditions by playing opposite them while they read their lines).

With their cast being rounded out with the likes of Terence Stamp, Ned Beatty, Harry Andrews, Susannah York, Valerie Perrine, Glenn Ford, Sarah Douglas and Jackie Cooper, it was time to find a way to make the Man of Steel appear to fly on screen, which was no small feat in itself.

John Barry was brought in as production designer and he lent his unique visual flair to the proceedings, in particular the planet Krypton. He saw the Kryptonians as an advanced race of beings living in a breathing, crystalline world. Geoffrey Unsworth called upon his vast experience as cinematographer to bring a unique look to film, the first half focussing on life on Krypton before shifting to the rolling wheat fields of Kansas next. Unsworth gives the early proceedings a muted pastel look, toned down, ushering an almost dreamlike quality. When Clark Kent arrives in Metropolis, the city has a harsher, grittier blue of reality.

At the 1979 Academy Awards, *Superman the Movie* was nominated in several categories, including special effects (which it rightly won). It was criminally overlooked when it came to cinematography and production design, much to Donner's chagrin. Sadly, Unsworth would pass away before *Superman* made it to the big screen, while Barry was to die at the too-young age of 44 shortly after its release.

As noted, the film won an Oscar for its effects, but it took a while to get them up to scratch. Just how did you make a man fly and make it look real? Many old school tricks were used to accomplish the feat. Chief among them was the classic man-on-a-wire technique, as seen in the *Peter Pan* stage play. This time, they had state of the art harness techniques that would give Superman the lift needed, and it took many months of trial and error to perfect this as a live-action effect. Motion control cameras were also used. These had been created chiefly for *Star Wars* which came out the year before. They were utilised in model shots using a fake Superman whizzing through the skies.

But the main effect was the classic front projection technique, wherein an actor stands (or in this case flies) in front of an image which is projected behind him. Technical effects expert Zoran Perisic had perfected the effect with a new front projection process which involved zoom lenses on both the camera (capturing the image) and the projector (providing the back plate).

The lenses were synchronised to focus together simultaneously in the same focal plane or direction. As the projection lens zoomed in, it shows a smaller image behind Reeve; while the lens focussing on Reeve zooms in at the same time and degree, giving the effect that the background image appears unaffected. While this happens, the camera lens trained on the actor gives the effect of him moving closer to the camera and away from the back plate. This whole process gives a fluid movement, tricking the eye into believing it is seeing motion and depth, with constant scale representation. Perisic called this process the Zoptic Effect and it has been used in many films since, including the *Superman* sequels.

But the biggest and best special effect used in the flying sequences has to be Christopher Reeve himself.

He sells the whole idea that he can really fly. His take off and landings are almost elegant in their execution, and he banks his body whilst in flight to make it look like he's literally riding wind currents and directing his own flight path. In real life, he was an accomplished glider pilot. Whether this gave him an understanding of flight and lift is open for conjecture, but he obviously looks like he belongs in the sky.

Compare the effect to today's standards. Actors in flying harnesses utilising the wirework effect for flight look as stiff as boards, even with all the computer enhancements we have now. It makes you appreciate even more the effort Reeve and the rigging crew put into the film to achieve such spectacular results. Add to that the fact that during the Metropolis scenes, where Superman first appears, Reeve is sometimes two hundred feet in the air...Yikes!

Another effect used is that of model miniatures. These were used in many scenes, from representing the filming

of the planet Krypton to the destruction of the Hoover Dam and the Golden Gate Bridge in San Francisco. Effects artist Derek Meddings, the man responsible for classic TV shows such as *Thunderbirds* and *Captain Scarlet*, brought his expertise to the production. Meddings' work has real scale and weight to it, and most of the time you question what's real and what's a miniature effect - he was that good! Unfortunately, when it came to the destruction of the dam during the main action sequence near the end of the picture, Meddings had to leave for pastures new, as he was contracted to do the next James Bond extravaganza. By then, production on *Superman* was well behind schedule. Another effects crew took over this particular miniature sequence. While it's competently done, it doesn't match what Meddings had previously achieved. It is quite jarring to see and is arguably one of the weaker parts of the film.

A bombastic spectacle like *Superman* needs an equally spectacular musical score to accompany it, and maestro extraordinaire John Williams composed the music and wielded the composer's baton in front of the London Symphony Orchestra. Williams had been responsible for previous musical delights on blockbusters such as *Jaws*, *Star Wars* and *Close Encounters of the Third Kind* and had wowed critics and audiences alike. He was a household name… and rightly so.

Jerry Goldsmith was initially asked to provide the score, as he had done a masterful job working with Donner on *The Omen*, but due to conflicting schedules he had to drop out. Williams was approached, and Donner couldn't believe his luck when he proved available and accepted the job.

The score generates the majesty needed to project the full power of the Man of Tomorrow onto the big screen. The opening title music and march actually cry out Superman's name. The various bombastic overtures and subtle character-driven themes are a delight to listen to. One of my personal favourites is when a teenage Clark, still back home in Smallville, races on foot alongside a speeding locomotive. You feel the raw power of the train through the music, rocketing down the track, only for it to be out horse-powered by the most powerful being on the planet!

John Williams has crafted many memorable themes over the years, from classic TV sci-fi like *Lost in Space* and *Land of the Giants* to the *Indiana Jones* films, but *Superman* seems to have more heart to it. This may be down to the sheer affection for one of America's favourite fictional characters that Donner insisted upon. Williams never fails to impress with his scores, but this theme always seemed to have something that little bit more…*super*… to it.

With all the technical difficulties to overcome (some of them never before attempted for a motion picture), no-one should have been surprised that production was running significantly behind schedule much to the Salkinds' impatience. This made the budget bloom and drastic decisions had to be made with the release date looming ever closer.

Both the Salkinds and Donner were by now being very frosty towards each other. Donner was taking all the heat, but didn't want the growing resentment to affect his actors. Something had to be done, and the decision was made to focus everything on completing the first picture. Shooting on the sequel came to a stop. It was also decided to put the ending of *Superman II* onto the ending of the first film, so scripts were re-jigged and the go-ahead was given.

Superman the Movie was finally released on December 15th, 1978 pretty much everywhere, and went on to enjoy international acclaim, breaking many box-office records along the way. It was Warner Bros' highest grossing films for many years.

When the entire hullabaloo had calmed down, it was time to return to work and finish *Superman II*, only this time it would be without Donner at the helm. The Salkinds in their infinite wisdom fired him and brought Richard Lester into the fold. They'd worked with him on the *Musketeer* films and he'd been acting as a sort of go-between for Donner and the Salkinds when their working relationship totally broke down.

The rest, as they say, is history. The original spawned three sequels, each weaker than its predecessor. There were a lot of reasons for this, but the main one was the lack of Donner's steady hand on the tiller. He seemed to understand the importance of the Man of Steel in American culture and just what exactly he represented.

Donner's *Superman* is a masterpiece in its own right, blending the romantic charm of classic Hollywood movies in their heyday with the action-packed blockbuster of the modern era. Although Superman hailed from a distant, long-dead planet and his dense Kryptonian physiognomy gave Clark Kent the power of a God, Donner *humanised* the character. He made him far more believable and relatable than the source material ever had.

The whole secret behind the Superman mythos is that he doesn't need to be relevant to the era he is currently interpreted in. Superman as a character needs to inspire the people of that era, and Donner fully understood this.

I don't know about other fans out there, but speaking personally, after seeing the film for the first time in 1978, it was the best Christmas present of that year. I believed Reeve *was* Superman. He embodied all that was just and right with the character.

And more importantly, I believed a man could really fly!

All I had to do to find him was look… up in the sky…

The Night Porter

by Ian Taylor

'Variety' described the 1974 movie *The Night Porter* (original title *Il portiere di notte*) as a "strange, brooding tale… a gritty look at concentration camp quirks but transposed to a strange drama." Elsewhere, you will find it described more helpfully as an Italian erotic psychological drama. Its themes of both sexual and sadomasochistic obsession have undoubtedly made the film controversial. Critics and general viewers have long been divided over its artistic worth.

The Night Porter is widely considered a Nazisploitation film, and this perhaps dooms it to being forever labelled a cult classic rather than simply a great piece of cinematic work. So, is it Nazisploitation or something more highbrow?

For me, *The Night Porter* - directed and co-written by Liliana Cavani, starring Dirk Bogarde and Charlotte Rampling, with supporting roles from the likes of Philippe Leroy and Gabriele Ferzetti - inarguably deserves more respect. Viewers need to put aside their concerns over a script which focuses on characters who have been shaped by the atrocities of the Second World War (in particular, the horrendous mistreatment of Jewish prisoners in the concentration camps). Put aside those concerns, take a step back, and think long and hard about what the film is trying to say. Ask yourself if any of this particularly horrible portion of history is in any way glorified. Then come back with a review…

The tale focuses on former German SS officer Max (Bogarde) and former camp detainee Lucia (Rampling) examining their relationship in the war years as well as in 1957 Vienna. An intimate and twisted relationship is resumed when they accidentally meet at the hotel where Lucia and her husband are guests. Max is the titular character, a concierge who works the night shift because he experiences shame in the daylight. It is clear neither of them has been able to escape from their dark past and both are mentally and emotionally scarred. Lucia, now a bored housewife whose husband frequently leaves her for work, is confused and shocked when memories of her life as a captive/plaything in a concentration camp are revived. This results in the strange, mutually dependent sexual relationship she had with Max being reawakened. Meanwhile, Max fears he will be outed as a war criminal and is scared Lucia may have purposely tracked him down. As their damaging partnership begins again, Max's old fellow Nazi comrades wish to confront her, and a bleak ending demonstrates that no-one is able to escape their terrible past.

It's a grim tale, to be sure, but always fascinating. It is certainly not a gratuitously exploitative fun fest. Bu for all the grimness, it has a fair amount of grandiose beauty thanks to Alfio Contini's cinematography which makes Vienna look beautifully epic. Danielle Paris' fine soundtrack emphasises the stunning architecture, and director Cavani brings to life a story and characters which intricately balance the dark and the light, the passion and the sickness.

The hotel location is amazing, carrying a real sense of opulence and decadence, something that is also reflected in certain guests and contrasts strikingly with the cold, clinical Max and the grubbiness of the behind-the-scenes 'services' he oversees. Bogarde is efficient and emotionless as the concierge, at least on the surface. Beneath it, he is cruel.

The non-linear structure of the script from director Cavani and Italo Moscati works perfectly in establishing characters and situations, then revealing (sometimes slowly, sometimes in shockingly blunt fashion) aspects of their past. It keeps the audience on their toes, constantly re-evaluating their thoughts and feelings about the characters. It is here, of course, that the Nazi/Jewish captive relationship of the Bogarde/Rampling characters is teased out, sometimes showing violence and fear, at other times passion and even tenderness. This structure ultimately prevents the viewer from making any instant value judgements. Or perhaps not... considering some of the harsh and often hysterical responses it has garnered. But the writer/director's cleverly fragmented approach successfully echoes the fragmented psyches and messed-up histories of the principal characters, and certainly helps to avoid the pulp fiction villain/victim presentation of genuinely exploitative movies such as *The Beast in Heat* or the *Ilsa* series. *The Night Porter* is really not done in such a way. The characters are nuanced and many-faceted, full of light and dark, and the flow of the text is broken with many flashbacks to highlight how both of the main characters' lives are ruptured by their mutual past.

But then, Liliana Cavani is a special kind of director and screenwriter. She came from a generation of Italian filmmakers that made a big impact with their work in the '70s, that most interesting of cinematic decades. Hailing from the northern region of Emilia-Romagna - an area well known for its beautiful seaside resorts, medieval cities and top gastronomy - Cavani shared her heritage with Federico Fellini, but also shared '70s success with exciting directors like Marco Bellocchio (*Victory March*, *The Seagull*), Bernardo Bertolucci (*The Conformist*, *Last Tango in Paris*) and Pier Paolo Pasolini (*The Decameron*, *The Canterbury Tales*). Of course, these directors were producing worthwhile work prior to the '70s, but they all absolutely shone during this particular era. Cavani had

been directing since 1961, mainly in television, and really started hitting her stride in the mid-to-late '60s. She typically dwelled on people and moments of historical importance, as in *Women of the Resistance* (1965), *Francis of Assisi* (1966) and *Galileo* (1968). But it was *The Night Porter* that raised her profile on an international level.

Cavani is patient in allowing the story to fully unfold. There is much establishing of character before Max and Lucia meet again in 1957. While their eventual reunion lacks the obvious 'fireworks', it is an intensely effective moment. Rampling conveys pain, horror and fear at first. These emotions are subtly conveyed, buttoned up, but there's something very truthful in the way this woman's painful secret is examined. We sense that her secret provokes in her feelings of shame and guilt (whether justified or not). Everything is there to be seen but is coolly played down. Bogarde remains calmly impassive, but his eyes give it all away. There is no melodramatic action at this point - no action at all, in fact. But soon there is a flashback showing rows of gloomy camp prisoners, with insufficient fight left to display even demonstrative unhappiness. There is nudity, but it is presented in drab, bleak discomfort, entirely avoiding titillation. It simply isn't that type of film, at least not in the main. The movie then progresses in parallel timelines, the war years and the late '50s, each strand moving forward our understanding of the peculiar relationship of Max and Lucia. These complex people needed to be played carefully and intelligently and, in Bogarde and Rampling, Cavani could hardly have chosen better actors for the job.

Dirk Bogarde was born with the grand name of Derek Jules Gaspard Ulric Niven van den Bogaerde on 28th March 1921, in London, the son of a newspaper arts editor and an actress. Starting on stage, he made his film debut as an extra in the George Formby comedy *Come on George!* in 1939 before the Second World War broke out and his career was interrupted. He joined the Queen's Royal Regiment as an officer, eventually earning the rank of Major. On returning to acting, he soon impressed in principal roles in the likes of a television adaption of the Patrick Hamilton play 'Rope' (1947) - a year before Alfred Hitchcock's superb big screen version - as well as *Once a Jolly Swagman* (1949) and *The Blue Lamp* (1950). By the '50s he had become a matinee idol, his good looks and ability to smoulder or perform comedy working to great effect in movies like Terence Fisher's brilliant drama *So Long at the Fair*, classic war movie *They Who Dare* (both 1950) and a trio of light-hearted romantic comedies in the popular *Doctor* series. An intelligent, thoughtful man, he also wrote seven best-selling volumes of memoirs, six novels and a collection of journalistic articles, mainly for the 'Daily Telegraph'. This deeper side became more and more apparent in the films he made following his time as a romantic lead for the Rank Organisation; the likes of

The Servant (for which he won a BAFTA), *Victim* and *Accident*. The '70s brought more work of a serious nature, such as *Death in Venice* (1971). By 1974, *The Night Porter* was far more in keeping with his output than the jolly, dreamy days of *Doctor in the House*.

One of Bogarde's great strengths, particularly in this project, was his ability to convey so much from beneath an impassive exterior, all with the slightest twitch of an eyebrow, a tightening of the lips or slight frown. His eyes spoke eloquently of many varied memories and emotions, and this worked perfectly in scenes such as those with his former wartime associate Bert (Amedeo Amodio). In an evocative sequence, we see Max acting as lighting operator in a hotel bedroom, seemingly emotionless as he uses a large spotlight to track the dancing of Bert. Milanese-born Amodio had trained at ballet school and later set himself up as a choreographer and dancer. Cavani would use him in two movies, *The Night Porter* being the first. His dancing is admirably haunting, suiting the sad performance in an empty room. It shows how these remnants of the Nazis are trapped by their past, confined in what they do. In fact, the finale results in Bert kneeling before Max in a picture that is suggestive of interrogator and detainee. This visual link to Max's past as an SS officer suddenly, yet logically, returns us to the '40s. Bert dances near naked in clinical, white surroundings, which marks a striking contrast to the dark room a decade later. Back then, there was also a bigger audience of Nazi officers. Immediately, both decadence and a lack of feeling is once more suggested. Cleverly, the war years are not depicted as being particularly rich or comfortable. Moments of pleasure (dancing, drinking, sex) are presented in places either spartan, cold or downright grubby. This is partially what separates the whole enterprise from Nazisploitation. There is clearly no glorification here.

On the other hand, the present is often sumptuously presented, and in itself this provides a startling juxtaposition. In the very slow, patient build-up to the inevitable resuming of relations between Max and Lucia, there is a night at the opera. There are long, meaningful looks as high art is performed on stage. Interspersed are flashbacks of base German officers using prisoners for sex. Max invasively inserts his fingers into the mouth of a younger, close-cropped, dead-eyed Lucia, a symbolic forced penetration. For all the high-class pursuits, rich living and grand surroundings, there are no happy faces in the '50s. Each timeline is bleak. The war has cast a shadow over everyone in the subsequent decade.

As director of photography, Alfio Contini shows us the almost embarrassing grandiosity but maintains a drab colour scheme that perfectly emphasises Cavani's story. Both past and present having been effectively established in tone and circumstance, Lucia finds herself left alone at the hotel as her husband leaves on business. Not only has the audience been provided with everything they need to inform them of what must now happen, they have also been encouraged to dread it. The director takes no chances though, opting to contrast the comfortable yet

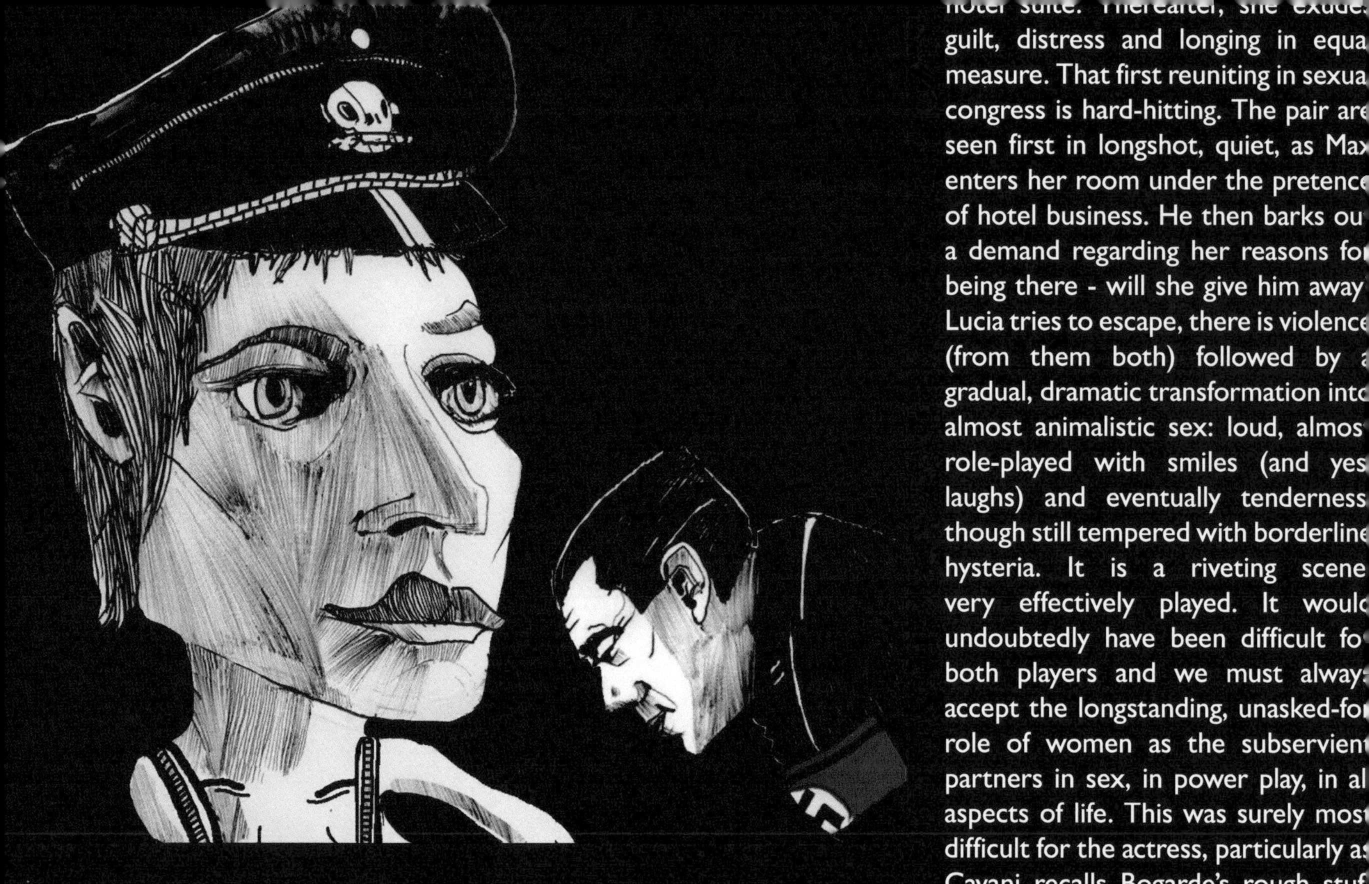

miserable present (as Lucia sits alone in the hotel bar) with the horror of Max swabbing her wounds in in the camp hospital of the past. And in a queasily disturbing moment, we are shown just how strange a turn the relationship between captor and captive is taking as the SS officer kisses the girl's hideous and bloody wounds better.

Charlotte Rampling excels at conveying the younger, dulled, shocked and abused Lucia, but also the older, healthier yet emotionally scarred version. The subtle distinctions between each are enhanced by useful comparisons. When the old character visits an expensive shop, she looks at a long, white dress and we are immediately transported back to a younger self having Max slip a simple, white smock over her head in the camp hospital. She is one and the same person; she remembers these events, they are with her still, and yet the emotions involved grow ever more ambiguous.

The actress was born Tessa Charlotte Rampling on 5th February 1946 in the English county of Essex and was schooled in exclusive establishments in both France and England. She was a model before taking up acting in the mid '60s and her earliest roles were in trendy pop culture titles such as The Beatles' movie *A Hard Day's Night* and director Richard Lester's further picture *The Knack… and How to Get It*. Despite the occasional lower-brow project such as the horror film *Asylum*, Rampling swiftly became known for her work in more serious productions, and her French education helped her to ease into European arthouse pics like Luchino Visconti's *The Damned* (1969) alongside Bogarde. Surprisingly enough, there are rumours that Cavani wasn't initially interested in having Rampling in the movie, but she is perfect in the role, visually, physically and emotively. Her acting ability allows her to show a lot through a little during the slow burn build-up to the final coming together of Lucia and Max in her darkened hotel suite. Thereafter, she exudes guilt, distress and longing in equal measure. That first reuniting in sexual congress is hard-hitting. The pair are seen first in longshot, quiet, as Max enters her room under the pretence of hotel business. He then barks out a demand regarding her reasons for being there - will she give him away? Lucia tries to escape, there is violence (from them both) followed by a gradual, dramatic transformation into almost animalistic sex: loud, almost role-played with smiles (and yes laughs) and eventually tenderness though still tempered with borderline hysteria. It is a riveting scene very effectively played. It would undoubtedly have been difficult for both players and we must always accept the longstanding, unasked-for role of women as the subservient partners in sex, in power play, in all aspects of life. This was surely most difficult for the actress, particularly as Cavani recalls Bogarde's rough stuff was decidedly 'method' and Rampling declined a further take. All artistic performance requires an opening up, an exposing of one's thoughts and feelings, a wearing of the heart on the sleeve and leaving oneself vulnerable. Here, Rampling is (at least partially) naked, bruised and pushing herself to emotional and physical places that she would have found more than difficult, and she aces it.

The comedown is hard-hitting too: the regret, the upset, all expertly and believably conveyed as she huddles foetus-like on the floor beneath a blanket. Bogarde tosses her a telegram from her husband, finishes off the hotel business conversation in a cool, clinical manner as befits a former SS officer and exits. It is raw, powerful, upsetting and thought-provoking, but never exploitative. Or, to put it another way, anyone getting their kicks from viewing such a scene might be better off seeking some therapy!

Cavani later reflected upon the misunderstandings of the film that led to such reviewers as Pauline Kael of the 'New Yorker' calling it: "humanly and aesthetically offensive." In November 2020, Cavani told Ryan Gilbey of 'The Guardian' that she was greatly displeased with the US distributor Joseph E. Levine for promoting the picture by playing up the negative reviews and general outrage. She told Gilbey: "It damaged the reputation of the film. It was seen as a sexual work and that's not at all what I wanted to do."

Clearly, there were other, deeper themes that were being overlooked, and surely anyone checking out the film in the hope of niche porn or gory action will be left puzzled and disappointed. Those looking for an intelligent work which examines the mental and emotional effects of persecution and domination (from both perspectives) or the way history shapes and stains those who lived through it will come away far more satisfied.

"Guilt complex is a disturbance of the psyche," claims a Nazi old boy at one point, and yes, *The Night Porter* is a scrutiny of the psychological effects of the Nazis and their victims after the event, of the concept of guilt (of both sufferer and perpetrator) even years later. Some of the Nazis want to speak out, to confess, to defend themselves. Bogarde doesn't want it all raked up again - enough to commit murder, in fact - but he finds that it does rear its ugly head once more, in unexpected ways. When Max says that he wants any witnesses left "in peace", to "forget", he means the likes of himself but a swift cut to Rampling shows that this cannot possibly happen.

The scenes of sexual activity are, like all elements of the main characters' lives, permanently tainted. They are presented in rooms that are as drab, and colours that are as muted, as the mood is dark. Arguably, the only scene that carries a genuine erotic charge is the iconic topless song/dance that Rampling performs in Nazi hat, trousers and braces and little else. It is certainly memorable, but there is still plenty of darkness involved to offset the sexuality of the sequence. It features brave playing from Rampling as we see Lucia perform for a room full of Nazis. Physically, it is easy to see why the actress was deemed perfect - her slim (bordering on thin with prominent ribs) figure and small breasts enhance the sense of a young innocent corrupted, a mistreated camp inmate. Lucia is shown to be a fragile figure, but at this moment she clearly holds the power as every eye in the room is on her. With her provocative dancing, her husky, almost ambivalent song and her very nakedness, she is dominant. Which feeds very smoothly into the key question in the Vienna of 1957, amidst the sex games between Max and Lucia… who is in control? Who is tormenting who? Who holds the power, he or she, as they attempt to find comfort in their sex games?

The intensity of this is amplified by the encroachment of Max's Nazi friends and the insidious gaslighting from Hans (an effectively calm and reasonable yet hateful performance from Gabriele Ferzetti). He presents Lucia as the guilty one, for disturbing the past and unfairly upsetting the ex-Nazi officers - she is bad for being a reminder! One of the most effective moments sees Hans interviewing/interrogating Lucia. He is impassive and relentless whilst offering a sickening voice of reason. Rampling, meanwhile is simply astonishing as she hides under a table, prowls on all fours, growls "go away" and finally hides in the bathroom.

Of course, it is essential that we are not offered the soft and dishonest option of a happy ending. That would betray the mood and the message. *The Night Porter* is always respectful in what it tries to do. It deserves more respect than it has traditionally received. It is not provocatively shocking Nazi porn in the *Salò, or the 120 Days of Sodom* mould, nor is it a cheap-looking and blatant exploitation movie. It is beautifully shot, cleverly structured, expertly directed and powerfully played.

Hopefully, it will continue to gain some of the respect it is owed. In July 2018, for example, it was selected to be screened in the 'Venice Classics' section at the 75th Venice International Film Festival.

Watership Down

by Eric McNaughton

"Long ago, the great Frith made the world. He made all the stars, and the world lived among the stars. Frith made all the animals and birds and, at first, made them all the same.
Now, among the animals was El-Ahrairah, the Prince of Rabbits. He had many friends, and they all ate grass together. But after a time, the rabbits wandered everywhere, multiplying and eating as they went.
Then Frith said to El-Ahrairah: "Prince Rabbit, if you cannot control your people, I shall find ways to control them."
But El-Ahrairah would not listen and said to Frith: "My people are the strongest in the world." This angered Frith, so he determined to get the better of El-Ahrairah. He gave a present to every animal and bird, making each one different from the rest. When the fox came, and others like the dog and cat, hawk and weasel, to each of them Frith gave a fierce desire to hunt and slay the children of El-Ahrairah."

I first read Richard Adams' 'Watership Down' around 1977. It quickly became one of my favourite books, and indeed remains in my top three of all-time (the others being 'Dracula' and 'Les Miserables'). Like George Orwell's 'Animal Farm' and Jonathan Swift's 'Gulliver's Travels', it can be read on two levels - as a childrens' adventure story about rabbits, or as a look at the human condition and how we face up to and conquer adversity.

It grew out of stories Adams used to tell his daughters Juliet and Rosamund on car journeys (fittingly, the book is dedicated to them). At their insistence, he began to write the various stories down… and 18 months later he had himself a novel. Wanting to make his characters as 'rabbit-like' as possible, he read a number of natural history books, most notably Ronald Lockley's 'The Private Life of the Rabbit'. Adams and Lockley eventually became friends, even undertaking a South Pole adventure together!

Adams tried unsuccessfully to drum up interest in his manuscript but was rejected by seven publishing houses before Rex Collings agreed to take a chance by publishing it. It was Collings who came up with the title 'Watership Down' (a real place, just south of the town of Newbury). Collings couldn't even pay an advance, and his friends and colleagues thought he was crazy to take on a text by an unknown writer featuring characters who were all rabbits. Luckily for us, Collings saw something in the story and it became an immediate hit, staying in the 'New York Times' bestseller chart for eight months where it peaked at number 1. World sales steadily built, and it was soon well on its way to selling more than 50 million copies in eighteen different languages. In fact, it would become the all-time best-selling title for the publisher Penguin.

For the story, Adams created a fictional language called lapine (derived from the French word for rabbit) and this carries over to the film version. Some examples are Elil (a term that refers to the natural enemies of rabbits - foxes, badgers, stoats, etc. - and also humans), Homba (a fox), Lendri (a badger), Hrududu (any motor vehicle), Silf (outside, outdoors) and Tharn (to be petrified with fear).

I was lucky enough to meet Adams once, back in 1980. We were both speakers at a rally in Trafalgar Square against the annual barbaric seal hunt in Newfoundland. I was excited to meet the author of one of my

favourite books, but that soon turned to disappointment when he told me: "If I found a rabbit in my garden eating my plants, I'd blow its bloody head off!" They do say you should never meet your heroes!

With the book proving a worldwide success, it was perhaps inevitable a movie version would be made. Producer Martin Rosen bought the film rights for £50,000. The budget was set at $2.4 million and production began in 1975. Originally it was set to be directed by John Hubley (and some of his work can still be seen in the finished product, most notably the opening tale of El-Ahrairah). Hubley was a fascinating character, a veteran animator who'd worked as a background artist on a few Walt Disney classics including *Snow White and the Seven Dwarfs* (1937), *Pinocchio* (1940), *Dumbo* (1941) and *Bambi* (1942). In 1949, he'd created the character Mr. Magoo, before he was blacklisted by the House Committee of Un-American Activities for refusing to cooperate with their communist 'witch-hunt'. After a falling out with Rosen, Hubley departed from the production. Rosen himself then took on directorial duties.

Anyone who expected a Disney-type cartoon about bunnies was in for a shock! I remember my sister asking me to look after her three kids one afternoon and I decided to treat them all with a trip to the cinema to see this new cartoon about rabbits. A few hours later, I handed three very traumatised children back to her and she swore never to trust me again! Indeed, the British Board of Film Classification is to this day receiving complaints about *Watership Down*. It seems strange that the film was given a U certificate in the UK considering the amount of death, gore and violence it depicts.

Rosen faced stiff resistance from the industry to get the movie financed and distributed. The story was thought too risky for any major studio, so it took him an age to find enough independent investors. He didn't even know how he was going to actually tell it on screen. He initially explored (then quickly dismissed) the idea of live action with costumes and prosthetics. He also considered using puppets (a Jim Henson approach) but soon realised this was also a non-starter. Eventually, he settled on the idea of animation but knew this decision would create preconceptions that *Watership Down* was a cartoon for children.

It opens with a wonderful origin story using simple woodcut-style animation and narrated by Michael Hordern (who was, at the time, the voice of Paddington Bear on TV). It is a creation myth for the world of rabbits, explaining how they came to be and why they had so many enemies ("the thousand"). The animation style changes when the story proper begins, with the rabbits being rendered in a very naturalistic and detailed way. It's a world away from the anthropomorphism of most cartoons, the only concessions being that the rabbits talk and show some facial expressions to convey emotions. The only other animals in the entire film that are able to speak are the farm cat Tab ("Can you run? I think not!") and Keehar the gull.

All the backgrounds were rendered in watercolours and based on the diagrams and maps in the original book. The locations, including Efrafa, the railway viaduct, the Sandleford warren and Watership Down itself, are

all based on real places in Hampshire. The editor Terry Rawlings camped out for a day and a night on the West Sussex downs to record a natural 'wildtrack'. He collected authentic sounds of the wind through the trees and grass, the actual rivers mentioned in the book, cars passing on the road and trains on the real railway bridge.

The film sticks fairly close to its source material, although some stuff is omitted to improve the pace. Having said that, in one case an incident from the book that is only mentioned in passing is expanded on in the film (the attack by the rats in the barn). When it comes to the darker aspects of the story, Rosen and his team don't hold back. Bigwig caught in the snare; Blackaver having his throat ripped out; the destruction of the Sandleford warren; the climactic battle between Bigwig and General Woundwort; and the attack of the dog are all portrayed unflinchingly. As noted earlier, when it was submitted to the BBFC it was passed with a U for Universal rating. At the time, the censors noted: "whilst the film may move children emotionally during its duration, it could not seriously trouble them once the spell of the story is broken and a U certificate is therefore quite appropriate." I have to say I'm not sure my sister would agree!

The cast of voice actors is exceptional. Among the main characters are John Hurt (Hazel), Richard Briers (Fiver), Ralph Richardson (Chief Rabbit), Roy Kinnear (Pipkin), Denholm Elliott (Cowslip), Hannah Gordon (Hyzenthlay), Harry Andrews (General Woundwort) and Zero Mostel (Keehar) in his last movie work.

The scoring was entrusted to the famous composer Malcolm Williamson (who was also Master of the Queen's Music). But when the deadline for the soundtrack arrived, he'd only actually got as far as composing the prelude and main title! Rosen had already hired a symphony orchestra,

recording studio and mixing technicians, so disaster seemed imminent. Luckily, Rosen's friend Jeff Wayne helped cover the costs by using the set up to record parts of his *War of the Worlds* album.

Angela Morey took over as the composer for *Watership Down*, reportedly scoring the complete soundtrack in less than three weeks. Her two previous scores, *The Little Prince* (1974) and *The Slipper and the Rose* (1976), had both been Oscar-nominated. It may have been a rush job, but her music here is highly effective.

Even with the film completed, Rosen couldn't find a distributor and had to do his own legwork to arrange the first few screenings. It was down to his investors to come up with the extra funds to make this possible and they managed to get it playing in five key London cinemas. There was very little associated publicity, yet in was instantly one of the top three films at the London box office. Then he started receiving interest from distributors and it was finally taken on by CIC. The movie opened on 19th October 1978 at the Empire in Leicester Square. Its US premiere was on 1st November the same year. In both the UK and the US, it garnered mostly positive reviews and was financially very successful (some investors received a 5000% return on their initial outlay).

There is no doubt its success was helped enormously by the release of the single *Bright Eyes*, sung by Art Garfunkel. Released in March 1979, six months after the movie had debuted, it went to number 1 in the charts and sold an astounding 1,155,000 copies, becoming the biggest selling single of its year. Ironically, the song almost didn't make it into the film. Composer Mike Batt (creator of *The Wombles*) had written three songs for *Watership Down* but two were dropped and it was touch and go if the third would make it. Even then, the CBS record label was unconvinced of its chart potential and didn't assign any promotional budget to its release. Without plugging, it stood little chance of significant sales. But when Rosen was invited onto the Terry Wogan radio show to talk about the film, he took a copy along with him and Wogan played it and the next week it topped the UK charts!

The power of *Watership Down* to affect its audience certainly hasn't diminished over the decades. A 2016 Easter Sunday screening by Channel 5 resulted in a Twitterstorm of indignation from the outraged parents of distressed children. They were *still* assuming it would be a cutesy Easter Bunny film where all the rabbits looked like Thumper! Even now, nothing can really prepare you for *Watership Down*'s hard-hitting content. It's doubtful a film like it would get made today. Rosen and his team went on to adapt Adams' 'The Plague Dogs' in 1982, making another superb, hard-hitting animated movie. Meanwhile *Watership Down* has been remade a number of times for television, generally with the harder aspects softened, but the original movie stands head and shoulders above them all. A superb cast, top notch animation and a producer/director who dared to take chances against all the odds combine to make it a true classic.

HAL ASHBY - THE GREATEST FORGOTTEN FILMMAKER OF THE SEVENTIES?

by John H. Foote

Post-production work on *Coming Home* (1978) was in full swing and one of its stars, Bruce Dern, was worried about looking like a nut job. Dern - a great actor who took his role as the damaged marine Bob Hyde very seriously - was concerned the film was going to portray him as a madman. He had, after all, shot John Wayne in *The Cowboys* (1972) and plotted to blow up 80,000 people at the Super Bowl in *Black Sunday* (1977). He was aware of the way the public perceived him. However, he had been in films long enough to know that the finished product came together in the editing room.

While visiting Hal Ashby at his home - where Ashby was busy working on the final cut of *Coming Home* - Dern explained his concerns to the director. Noting his apprehension, Ashby motioned the actor to the screen of the editing machine and asked him to watch. Dern sat and surveyed the climactic scenes juxtaposed against each other. His wife, portrayed by Jane Fonda, asks if he wants to barbecue some steaks, commenting that it must be a long time since he ran a BBQ. The slight smile on Dern's face suggests he has burned other things in Vietnam. We cut to Luke Martin (Jon Voight), paralyzed from the waist down during the combat, as he speaks to a group of high school students who might or might not be ready for what he has to say. Bob walks out onto the beach and begins undressing, shoes first, socks, then his uniform, working his way down. On the soundtrack, Tim Buckley's song *Once I Was* begins softly. We move back and forth between Luke's speech and Bob undressing. *"Once I was a soldier…and I fought on foreign sands for you,"* sings Buckley in his mournful tone. Bob, finally naked, uniform placed absurdly neatly on the sand, runs into the ocean and swims strongly out to sea. Luke tells the kids: "I did a lot of shit over there I find fucking hard to live with." Meanwhile, Bob swims out farther - to his death.

Stunned by what he had just seen, Dern grabbed Ashby in a tight embrace and kissed his cheek, thanking him. Tears flowed freely down the actor's face as his esteem for his filmmaker soared through the roof. Once again, Ashby had proven himself a great film editor, a gifted director and an artist who truly loved actors.

Oddly, when the great directors and their films of the '70s are discussed, only in recent years has Ashby become part of that conversation. For thirty years, it was as though he had been erased or at best neglected. The fact is his work in the '70s was sublime. Seven great achievements… at least three towering films. Nominated for Best Director for *Coming Home*, he deserved nominating for at least three others but sadly it didn't happen. He *was* an Oscar winner, but for his film editing on *In the Heat of the Night* (1967). Ashby himself would direct two Best Picture nominees and once be nominated for Best Director. He would also guide ten actors to Oscar nominations, with four of them winning the coveted golden statuette. But, outrageously, the man himself would never be crowned Best Director.

He had befriended Norman Jewison while working on the lot, and Jewison sought him to edit *The Cincinnati Kid* (1965) and a lifelong friendship was forged. Hired to cut *In the Heat of the Night*, Ashby impressed Jewison with his work ethic and the fact that he listened to everyone regardless of how heavily they were involved in the film. If he did not care for what they said, he simply disregarded it without fuss. He was never one for confrontation.

He often dressed in hippie garb (his everyday apparel) - love beads, torn jeans, a T-shirt, long straggly hair and an equally long beard. His face was a near-constant smile and the aroma of marijuana surrounded him. He did not look like a film director. He resembled one of the crew, an over-thirty hippy enjoying the newfound freedoms of the era. He loved making movies, the whole creative process. He would often stop shooting to remind his cast and crew how truly blessed they were to do what they were doing. While making *Coming Home*, he and Jon Voight were in the middle of discussing a scene when Ashby broke from the conversation and said: "Isn't this great? This is a great day, man. Here we are on a movie set, making art, making something special. Is it not a great thing, Jon?" Voight never forgot those words. The actor talks often of how Ashby knew when he had realism on screen. Voight talks about the opening of *Coming Home*, where a group of real-life Vietnam vets were permitted to just speak about their experiences of war. Voight was on a stretcher in the background, listening, waiting to break in with his line. He never does; the camera instead closes in on him as he listens and reacts to what he is hearing. Both he and Ashby knew they had captured something special without Voight uttering a word. They embraced one another and moved on.

Ashby loved his actors. Ruth Gordon, Bud Cort, Jack Nicholson, Randy Quaid, Warren Beatty, Jack Warden, Goldie Hawn, Julie Christie, David Carradine, Jon Voight, Jane Fonda, Bruce Dern, Penelope Milford, Peter Sellers, Shirley MacLaine and Melvyn Douglas spoke highly of him. He always encouraged them to talk, to bring him their ideas, *all* their ideas - even the crazy ones - because they might be golden. No-one ever had a bad idea on an Ashby set because he valued everything they suggested

and encouraged everyone to speak up. Ashby once said: "I don't visualize myself as 'the boss'. What I try to do is get as much creativity as possible from everyone I'm working with."

It has been suggested that because he was an editor (one of the best, in fact), he was already thinking how to cut the film in his head while shooting. He knew that the real finished product would soar or plummet in the editing room.

When the great directors of the '70s are discussed, the Americans who get mentioned most are Scorsese, Spielberg, Lucas, De Palma and Coppola. While they did indeed dominate the decade with extraordinary work, there are plenty of others who, in hindsight, made equally great films. Alan J. Pakula with *Klute* (1971), *The Parallax View* (1974) and *All the President's Men* (1976); Sidney Lumet with *Serpico* (1973), *Dog Day Afternoon* (1975) and *Network* (1976); Sydney Pollack with *Jeremiah Johnson* (1972), *The Way We Were* (1973) and *The Electric Horseman* (1979); William Friedkin with *The French Connection* (1971) and *The Exorcist* (1973). Ashby's filmography is also exceptional.

He helmed seven films in the '70s, four among the very best of the decade, those being *The Last Detail* (1973), *Shampoo* (1975), *Coming Home* (1978) (which remains his masterpiece, I think) and *Being There* (1979), a mesmerizing whimsical film about a simple-minded man rising to a position of great power in the United States. How prophetic! How perfect! His other three were well reviewed and interesting pictures: *The Landlord* (1970), his first film, which already displayed his gift for neo-realism; the wonderfully unusual *Harold and Maude* (1971); and *Bound for Glory* (1976) which was Oscar-nominated for Best Picture.

Let's explore each in the order they were made.

The Landlord (1970)

After speaking with his good friend Norman Jewison about his desire to direct, Jewison saw to it Ashby would get his chance with *The Landlord*, a gritty low budget film which allowed him to develop his style. He was deeply concerned with humanity. That was what he chose to explore - not only in his first film, but in everything he directed in the '70s.

This first film deals with a young man born into privilege and wealth who is given an apartment building to operate. Once there, he realizes it is a slum and most of his renters are far below the poverty line. Many of them are also black. Against his better judgement, he becomes friends with his tenants, and, though he could sell and move on, he decides to remain and fix the place up ensuring they have a decent and safe place to live.

Beau Bridges gives a fine performance as Elgar, the young man born into wealth, and Lee Grant was Oscar-nominated for her performance as Joyce, his mother. The narrative explores the connection, or lack of, between the black community and their white landlord. The blacks do not expect what they get with Elgar. He enters a relationship with a light-skinned young black woman, Lanie (Marki Bey), but they are under strain from the start because he has fathered a child with Fanny (Diana Sands) during a brief affair. Fanny gives up the child, but Elgar gains custody. He finds a way to continue his relationship with Lanie, providing the child with a family.

Ashby's gifts with actors are apparent in the film. He draws outstanding performances from Bridges (who would soon be eclipsed by his brother Jeff), Lou Gossett Jr. as a black activist named Copee, and the aforementioned Lee Grant. *The Landlord* drew solid reviews from the critics in North America, who took note of the director's neo-realistic style, and it was placed on many ten best lists in 1970.

No question, his career as an editor was over, and he had become a filmmaker.

Harold and Maude (1971)

An exquisite, offbeat romance and daring black comedy with an outstanding performance from Ruth Gordon (a recent Oscar winner for *Rosemary's Baby*), Ashby's *Harold and Maude* would become one of the most popular cult films of the decade and a regular at repertory cinemas. Though many aspects of it are somber, it rings of truth and is as funny and beautiful as it is dark.

Age means nothing, we discover, when one falls in love. Harold (Bud Cort), a deeply confused youth, is constantly staging fake suicides to gauge the reactions from his family, who are by now used to the antics of their very odd family member. Encountering Maude (Gordon) at a funeral, he finds she is a survivor of the Holocaust and, at 79 years of age, more than fifty years his senior. They quickly become firm friends. Ruth is a force of nature, fearless, wanting to do everything she can before she dies. Her time in a Nazi prison camp has taught her it is important to live life to the fullest. She tries to impart this to Harold. Knowing she has little time to do so, Ruth gets moving.

What she does not see coming it that Harold falls in love with her. Not as a friend - but head-over-heels, romantic, sexual love.

Ruth is carefree and thinks nothing about breaking the law. She steals what she wants and lives in a broken-down railroad car. She is a true hippy at the age of 79. Her sunny view of life stuns Harold and begins to rub off. He announces at a party given at his family's home that he will marry Maude, much to their disgust. But while dancing, Maude reveals her surprise to Harold and gift to herself - she has ingested sleeping pills and suspects she will be dead by midnight. A life-force such as Maude cannot help but rub off on Harold, and he emerges from their relationship altered somehow. He is ready to live to the full, with no apologies or reservations about who he is or what he wants.

Was the studio afraid of *Harold and Maude*? Indeed they were, because it was so different and none of the execs were sure how to market it. Nor did they know what audiences would think. In a sense they buried the film, and were shocked when those who saw it loved it.

In hindsight, there is no question Gordon deserved an Academy Award nomination as Maude, giving the finest performance of her impressive career. She is luminous, beautiful in a way we have rarely seen in a film, radiant on the inside and shining on the out. Their offbeat love story is as surprising as any film in the decade. It is acted with

such purity and beauty you cannot look away from the screen. Cort is wonderful as Harold, the gloomy young man who wants to get a reaction out of his mother - a real, honest reaction - but has worn her down with his antics. Maude arrives in his life just in time, and helps him see that life is indeed worth living and there is beauty in the smallest wonders all around you. The true wonder of the film is Maude.

Superb performances dominate *Harold and Maude*, furthering Ashby's standing in the industry as an actor's director. But the best was still to come.

The Last Detail (1973)

As Billy 'Badass' Buddusky, Jack Nicholson gives one of his greatest early performances. After exploding into the forefront of American actors with fine work in *Easy Rider* (1969) and *Five Easy Pieces* (1970), Nicholson was the actor of the moment, that rare type who connected with both men and women, and was able to walk the fine line between being a movie star and genuine actor. He and Ashby journeyed to Toronto in Canada to make *The Last Detail*, shooting in and around Regent Park, a housing project that became a ghetto in the '80s and beyond but looked enough like navy barracks to pass for one on screen.

The film's premise is deceptive and rather simple. Two marines are assigned to escort Meadows (Randy Quaid), a younger marine, to the brig (jail) for stealing a donation box. They think this will be an easy bit of fun while they await their next orders. They simply need to drop the kid off and the rest of the time is all theirs to party hard. Billy (Nicholson) and fellow Navy lifer Mulhall (Otis Young) think the kid is being harshly punished for a relatively petty crime. He has been sentenced to eight long years for stealing just forty dollars. The severity of his sentence might be because Meadows stole it out of a favorite charity of his commanding officer.

Given a week to deliver the boy to jail, Billy and Mulhall realize they have a few days before they have to be at their destination. They notice how shy and terribly naïve Meadows is, so they decide to show him a good time before his jail term begins. Despite their initial resentment of the detail to which they have been assigned, they find themselves liking Meadows. Even after discovering he is a natural thief, they decide to show him a good time before he is banged up. The rest of the movie follows the events as they lead the young guy to jail via a series of new experiences and hedonistic adventures.

Met with excellent reviews, *The Last Detail* was an immediate success despite studio concerns about the incredible amount of coarse language it contains. Ashby knew, having visited naval bases for his research, that the vernacular of sailors could be profane and very salty. Writer Robert Towne captures their life and language to perfection.

And Nicholson? Such a towering performance as Billy, digging into the role deep, living it, becoming this badass navy lifer with such intensity that one look at him tells us everything we need to know. The actor would win the Best Actor prize at the Cannes Film Festival, where the picture was widely praised, as well as a Best Actor Award from the National Society of Film Critics. *The Last Detail* was

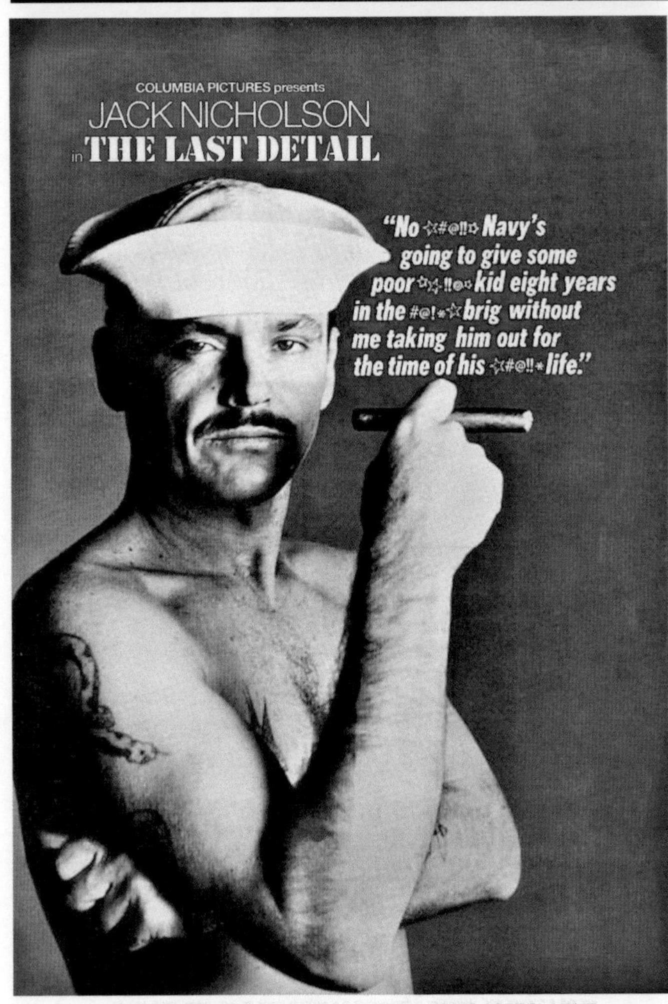

nominated for three Academy Awards too - Nicholson as Best Actor, Randy Quaid as Best Supporting Actor and Robert Towne for his superb screenplay.

Ashby's direction captures the journey of the sailors with authentic documentary-like realism. There are very few artistic flourishes, the simplicity of his directing being artistry enough. And in working with one of the cinema's greatest actors, Ashby discovered he had made a loyal friend.

Busted in Canada for carrying marijuana, the studio considered firing Ashby. But it was Nicholson who made it clear that Ashby stayed at the helm or he would walk. For the rest of the '70s they tried to find another project to do together… but it never came to pass. *The Last Detail* remains one of Ashby's greatest films. Once again, he sees and explores the humanity within the work, and ends up creating a compelling character drama *par excellence*.

Shampoo (1975)

This is a strange film for Ashby because he was specifically brought in by star Warren Beatty to helm it. Questions have since arisen regarding just how much directing Ashby actually did. After producing *Bonnie and Clyde* (1967) to great acclaim and substantial box office rewards, Beatty had his eye on directing a film. Paul Newman had directed *Rachel, Rachel* (1968) and won the New York Film Critics Award as Best Director but was left out of the Oscar nominations. Beatty felt if Newman could do it, he could too.

It might have behooved the actor to turn the film over to Ashby and just watch and learn. Beatty, of course, would go on to be an excellent director, winning an Academy Award and a Directors Guild Award for *Reds* (1981), his masterpiece about the Russian Revolution. Rumors state Ashby often sat on the sidelines during the filming of *Shampoo* while Beatty discussed scenes with the writer Robert Towne and many of the actors. There was no secret that this was Beatty's show. Ashby was there to more or less block out the scenes for the camera, and even then Beatty often overruled him. It has been stated that Beatty treated Ashby very shabbily and felt terrible about it for years to come. They became best friends after the shoot, but never again worked together.

Set in 1968, when Richard Nixon was elected President of The United States and Robert Kennedy was assassinated, the film explores the political unrest in the country. Yet, first and foremost, it is a dazzling character study of George (Beatty), the stud hairdresser who is brilliant with

hair and even better at bedding the multitude of women whose locks he styles. Old, middle aged, young, married, single, widowed, it does not matter to George because he loves giving pleasure, be it by styling their hair or thrilling them between the sheets. No movie Beatty made before or after so perfectly plays to his persona offscreen or the image he had carefully cultivated for himself.

The film is an intelligent look at politics in California and the State's importance in determining the presidency. But politics is always in the background, behind the Beatty story, which is often very funny and sometimes even moving. What emerges very smartly is a study of sexual politics. When George learns his promiscuous antics are ruining lives, he wakes up and decides to try to be a better man.

Though one might think *Shampoo* is a deep satire of the times, I am not so sure. I think, more than anything, it is a satire on the love life of Warren Beatty, who was at the time well known as a lover to countless women in Hollywood and around the globe. Despite a superb screenplay and strong performances, the picture never elevates to anything other than what it is - a study of Beatty's sexual prowess.

Beatty is terrific playing more-or-less himself. And man, does he look the epitome of cool on a motorcycle! Meanwhile, Julie Christie, Lee Grant, Goldie Hawn and a young Carrie Fisher are excellent as the many women George sleeps with. The ever-wonderful character actor Jack Warden is there too, and is his customary excellent self.

It's all very funny and sharp, for sure, but lacks the humanity with which Ashby tended to infuse his films. Though undoubtedly a good movie - sometimes very good - one can't help but notice that Ashby's directorial expertise is somewhat underused.

Bound for Glory (1976)

One of five Academy Award nominees for Best Picture in 1976, *Bound for Glory* was among the films tragically bested by *Rocky*, the Cinderella story about a boxer finding redemption and love in the ring and out. Sylvester Stallone's film caught the imagination of the American public and became a monster hit, and was nominated for ten Academy Awards. Going into Oscar night, did anyone seriously think it had a chance of winning? I know I certainly did not. The Best Picture nominees were *All the President's Men*, *Bound for Glory*, *Network*, *Taxi Driver* and *Rocky*. A strong line-up indeed, including three of the very greatest films of the decade. As we all know, *Rocky* did indeed win - for me, a terrible choice on the part of the Academy... but by 1976, we were used to it.

Ashby's *Bound for Glory* is a very fine film, beautifully crafted, capturing the details of the Great Depression to perfection with scenes often resembling the photographs

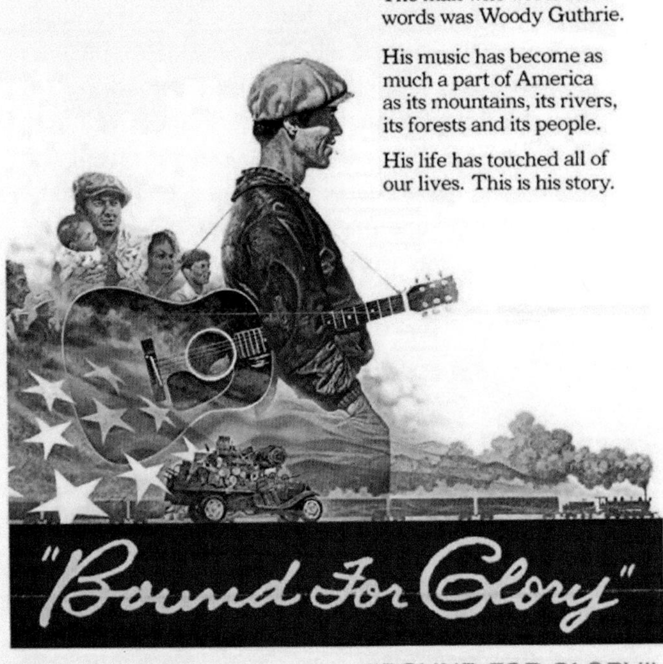

of the time. Hailed as a biography of the great folk singer Woody Guthrie (who fought social repression with song), Ashby captures the spirit and soul of Guthrie in his film. The greatest obstacle he had to overcome was casting. Who could play the folk singer? Who possessed the quiet power and dignity to step into the role? Jack Nicholson was too busy but did like the script and wanted to work with Ashby again, but two other films had him distracted, one of them with Marlon Brando, *The Missouri Breaks* (1976). Richard Dreyfuss was considered for the part, as was a young Martin Sheen. However, it was the distant, often distracted David Carradine who caught Ashby's eye. What Ashby liked about Carradine was that it did not really matter to him that this was a big studio production that could further his career. He did not care about the ramifications of a huge hit. His life was just fine as it was. Ashby loved Carradine's attitude and, against howls of protest from the studio, he cast the laid-back star as Woody Guthrie. The role did not make a star of the actor who, to this day, remains best remembered as Caine in the TV series *Kung Fu* and more recently as Bill in Tarantino's *Kill Bill* duo (2003/04).

As Guthrie, Carradine captures the essence of a man who sings about his deep love for America. He warbles darkly and tragically about working men and how they were oppressed during the Great Depression. We watch Guthrie touring America, riding the rails, walking and talking with the people he sings about, finding inspiration for his songs everywhere he goes.

Where the film struggles is in its exploration of what Guthrie really wants from his art and music. What were the deep reasons behind his song writing? Carradine's primary goal within the context of the film is to ask what his character wants. What drives him? We see him reacting to the injustices being poured on the common man, but what does he truly want to do about it? I'm inclined to suspect it was something much deeper than just writing music. He seemed to cling to the hope that his music and songs might somehow unite the nation, but this is not really explored within the film nor Carradine's performance. This raises questions about the limitations of Carradine as a performer. One suspects a better actor might have elevated *Bound for Glory* to being a great film, a film for the ages.

Bound for Glory was nominated for six Academy Awards, including Best Picture. It won two - Best Cinematography and Best Song Score (an award no longer given). Despite the Best Picture nomination, Ashby was ignored as Best Director. He did receive a Golden Globe nomination as Best Director, though.

The cinematography received deservedly high praise, earning, in addition to the Academy Award, other accolades from the Los Angeles Film Critics Association and the National Society of Film Critics. It certainly is a great-looking film, that's for sure.

Coming Home (1978)

Coming Home is Ashby's masterpiece, his finest work, and the film above all others for which he deserved to win an Oscar for Best Director and Best Picture. Instead, we watched Michael Cimino win both awards for *The Deer Hunter* (1978) a film predicated on the lies of a director who would prove himself to be a self-destructive egotist.

Coming Home was the brainchild of Jane Fonda who made it known she wanted to make a film about veterans returning from the unimaginable hell they had experienced. It was unlike any major film about the war experience, except *The Best Years of Our Lives* (1946), which beautifully and poetically dealt with the aftermath of WWII. Fonda wanted to make a picture which explored the intense trauma of the Americans who came home to be forgotten by their government and families.

Fonda would obviously portray the lead female role, leaving two plum male roles to cast. Ashby was by this time involved in the project as director. His first choice for Luke Martin, the paralyzed veteran, was Jack Nicholson but he turned it down. Others declining the role included Sylvester Stallone and

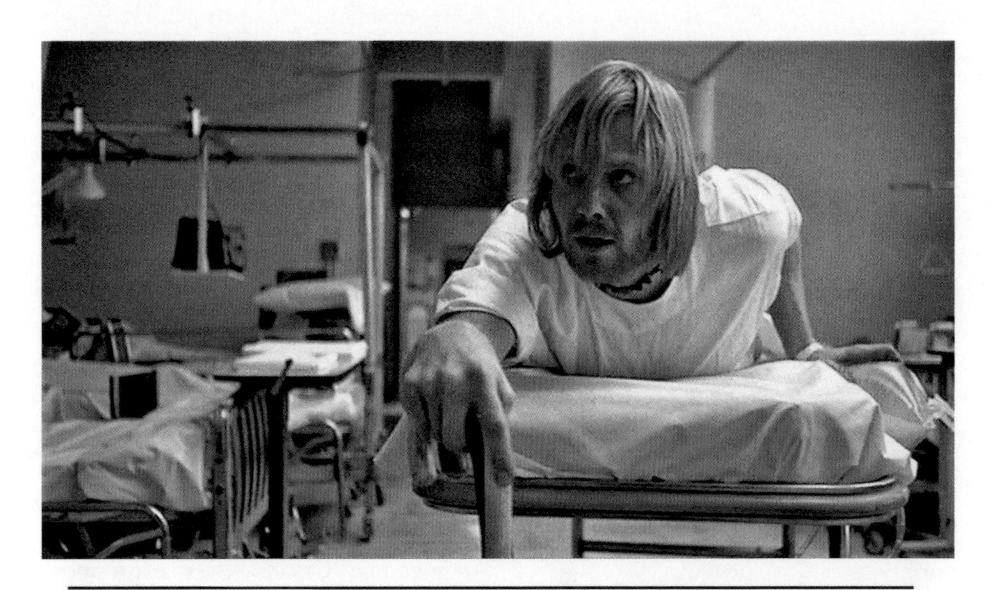

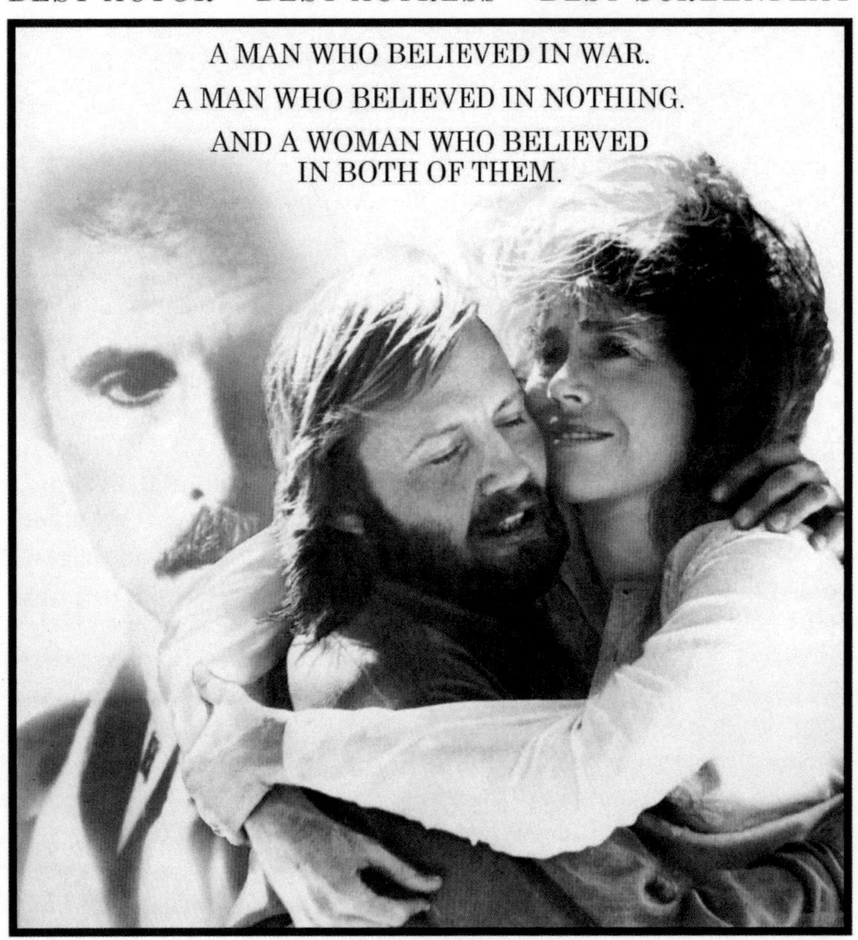

Martin Sheen. Jon Voight, however, knew what the film could mean, and grabbed the part. Bruce Dern had also been interested in portraying Luke, but instead happily accepted the part of Bob Hyde, husband of Fonda's character, Sally.

Bob is a hawk, a military lifer who cannot wait to get Vietnam and start killing gooks. He and Sally have been married a few years. He is clearly the alpha in the relationship, but sex between them is terrible with Sally never satisfied. When she takes a job at the Veteran's Hospital, she encounters Luke, a young man she knew in high school, now paralyzed from the waist down. She sees him often humiliated and, though she tries to get more funding for the men, she is rebuked. She and Luke engage in gentle flirting and seem to end up at the same places. When one of Luke's friends, a young man damaged by the war, kills himself, Luke chains himself to the gates of the military and is arrested. Sally bails him out and asks him to spend the night with her, beginning their affair and her sexual awakening (as she experiences her first orgasm).

When Sally visits Bob in Hong Kong, she sees a very different man than the one who left her in California. He is darker, haunted - the war is breaking him into pieces. He walks in circles in their hotel room talking about his men gleefully chopping off the heads of the Viet Cong "because that is what they're into." Returning home, Sally and Luke set up house together on the beach, with the specter of Bob hanging over them, unseen but always present.

When he returns home, Bob is a shell of the man who left. Angry, distant and explosive, he is a human time bomb about to go off. Informed by the army of his wife's affair, he comes at Sally with a weapon, but Luke intervenes reminding him that she loves him. Despite the fury with which Bob came into the scene, murder on the mind, he relents and gently puts the gun down.

The film ends with that scene Ashby proudly showed Dern when the actor was worried about being depicted as some sort of crazy, demented villain. With the horrors of Vietnam too much to bear, he swims into the sea to escape the pain. Meanwhile Luke advises young men to avoid the war at all costs: "there is a choice to be made."

Coming Home opened in the spring of 1978 and, despite very strong reviews, did little business. However, sensing potential Oscar nominations, the studio re-released it in December just as *The Deer Hunter* was being pre-screened for the press. The awards began piling up for Jon Voight as Best Actor from the LA Film Critics Association and the New York Film Critics. The Golden Globes honored both Voight and Fonda for lead actor and actress and, when the Oscar nominations were announced, the film was nominated eight times, including Best Picture and the long overdue shot at a Best Director award for Ashby.

The lies about *The Deer Hunter*'s origin were not yet known when voting for the awards took place. If they had been, I think the Oscars might have had a very different result. *The Deer Hunter* won five in all (Best Picture and Best Director among them) while *Coming Home* took three - Best Actor, Actress and Original Screenplay. In hindsight, I'm convinced Ashby should have won Best Director. The film itself deserved to be crowned Best Picture and Dern should have got the Supporting Actor award. As brilliant as Voight is, the heart of the film is Dern, a man truly broken by the war. Ashby understood this the moment he read the screenplay.

The legacy of *Coming Home* has become stronger as the years have slipped by. Though *Apocalypse Now* (1979) towers over all films made about Vietnam - maybe above all other films about war - *Coming Home* is right up there too, despite not showing a single combat scene. We see the terrible scars on the minds of Bob, Luke and the sad, guitar-playing teenager who kills himself with a needle full of air.

"The man went out," says a character.

Right. Just as Bob Hyde went out for a swim.

This is a stunning masterpiece, with Ashby directing at a level he had never attained before.

Being There (1979)

Ashby's last great film of the decade was *Being There*, which today seems more timely and urgent than ever. It asks: can a simpleton run a country? Our generation watched George W. Bush try to run the United States and, later, Donald Trump bumbled and lied his way through his presidency, finally committing insurrection on his own people in the hope of overruling the election in which he was defeated after four controversial years.

Being There was based on a novel by Jerzy Kosinski, who would later be known for his performance in Warren Beatty's *Reds* (1981) as Simoneov, a Russian leader under Lenin. The moment Ashby read it he knew he must direct the screen version. He had been in discussions to direct the adaptation of *Ragtime* (1981) from the sprawling E.L. Doctorow book but chose to go with *Being There*. In a stroke of genius, he cast the wraithlike Peter Sellers as Chance, a simple-minded groundskeeper for a wealthy man who has allowed Chance to grow up in his home. An orphan, Chance knows nothing of the outside world other than what he has seen on television.

The death of his elderly employer leaves Chance homeless and forced to go into a world he does not know or understand. A wealthy woman, Eve (Shirley MacLaine), is riding in a limo that injures Chance, so she takes him home. Her house is a massive mansion and her husband is revealed to be a wealthy man, Rand (Melvyn Douglas), who is much older than she and very close to the President. No one realizes anything is off about Chance. He is treated as a guest and given his own room in which to recover, a massive bedroom complete with a television. When asked about important foreign policies by some of the President's advisors and the President himself (Jack Warden), Chance answers in plant metaphors. He tells the men that if the roots are not harmed all will be well. They instantly take him for a political genius, and at that moment he becomes an important friend and advisor to the President. Meanwhile, Eve has fallen head-over-heels for Chance. When she throws herself at him, he informs her: "I like to watch", so she falls to the floor and masturbates herself to orgasm while he obliviously watches television. His fame grows and he continues to answer difficult questions in metaphors. While all the while he speaks of the garden, those listening believe he is talking about the economy.

Mr. Rand is very ill and asks Chance to take care of Eve when he dies, which of course he eventually does. It is at the old man's funeral that the idea to put Chance into the presidential race begins.

The final shot of the film, audacious and daring, shows Chance out for a walk on the grounds. He walks across a pond and stops to dip his umbrella in to find the bottom, then continues walking right across the water to the house.

A miracle indeed.

Being There was among the best films of 1979, hailed largely for the profoundly brilliant performance of Sellers, never better than as Chance. His bemused look masks the fact he understands only the basic questions they ask him, and his answers are taken as profound and truthful. Sellers dominates with his superb performance, while Douglas, MacLaine and Warden offer great support. In fact, the elderly Douglas won the Academy Award for Best Supporting Actor when many thought Robert Duvall should have got it for his fire-breathing colonel in *Apocalypse Now*.

Being There should have been a Best Picture and Best Director nominee but alas, it did not come to pass. Ashby finds the perfect tone in this superb satire, offering a touch of very black comedy by suggesting a simple-minded man could rise to the world's most powerful position.

Once again, the director demonstrates his brilliance with actors, gently guiding them all the way to the polished finished product. He listened where other director would not; he welcomed collaboration because he was egoless. Too few filmmakers realize that directors - indeed, anyone creating - needs to leave their ego at the door when working and encouraging collaboration of any kind.

One of the greatest political comedies ever made, *Being There* was the last classic made by one of the '70's finest filmmakers.

To be blunt, the studios chewed Ashby up and spat him out when they no longer needed him. Oh, he directed through the '80s, but it was mainly lightweight material, or films for TV, even a documentary. He was preparing to direct *Tootsie* (1982) but was replaced, and seemed to know then his time in Hollywood was finished. When he was diagnosed with pancreatic cancer that had spread to his liver and lungs, he died a horribly painful death. The many actors he had guided were frequent visitors. Warren Beatty came every day if he could and Jack Nicholson visited frequently too. Many others dropped in to comfort their beloved Hal on his hospital deathbed. When he passed away, we lost one of the greatest directors in the history of cinema.

At the Toronto International Film Festival, after a screening of *The Descendants* (2011) - directed by Alexander Payne and featuring George Clooney - I interviewed both men. Asking Payne who his influences were, he answered without hesitation: "Oh, without question Hal Ashby." Clooney smiled and answered: "There are a few, Lumet, Pakula and, of course, Hal Ashby. No-one captured humanity like Ashby did."

True words.

RABID DOGS

A Mario Bava Film So Very Different From His Others

by David Flack

When the subject of Italian film directors comes up, I find many accolades seem to be showered upon the likes of Lucio Fulci and Dario Argento. But another name interests me more - the unheralded genius Mario Bava. His body of work encompasses various genres, but horror was undoubtedly the main one. As a big fan of his films, my Top 5 list would look something like this:

1. *Black Sabbath* (1963)
2. *The Whip and the Body* (1963)
3. *Lisa and the Devil* (1973)
4. *Rabid Dogs* (1974)
5. *Black Sunday* (1960)

In this article, I'll be concentrating on number 4 from that list.

Rabid Dogs is unlike any other Bava film. It falls within the crime genre which he'd touched on in the crime/supervillain/comic-book entry *Danger: Diabolik* in 1968. This one, however, is far different in tone. *Rabid Dogs* (Italian title *Canni Arrabbiati*) is raw, violent, grim and full of incredibly tense scenes. Unusually for Bava (though not for the crime films of the time), it is peppered with coarse language, especially during the first half. The F-word is used liberally and, more surprisingly, the harsher C-word is uttered at one point. Watching the Italian version with English subtitles somehow makes this more shocking, probably because you see the words written down and therefore notice them more. Similarly explicit language was heard in *House of Exorcism*, a terrible, ill-advised re-edit of *Lisa and the Devil* (but, to be frank, I don't even count that as a Bava film in the true sense, as he was coerced into cobbling it together by rejigging footage from the other film).

Rabid Dogs was completed in 1974 but disaster struck when one of the film's backers died of a sudden heart attack. It went into bankruptcy proceedings and sat gathering dust on the shelf until 1996, when lead actress Lea Lander (along with others) helped finance a belated video release. Incredibly, this was 16 years after Bava's death. He had made the film to show he could compete in the extremely popular *poliziottesco* (crime drama) stakes. He certainly proved his point, as this is one of the best in the genre, and it's rather sad to reflect that he didn't get to experience the praise and acclaim his film deserved during his lifetime.

The story opens with a gang of four men carrying out the violent robbery of a pharmaceutical company's payroll. They show little regard for human life and callously stab a man to death. They make a break for it but one of them, their driver, is shot and killed in the getaway. The police, of course, are in pursuit.

The car breaks down and the remaining three criminals - leader Dottore aka Doc (Maurice Poli), Bisturi aka Blade (Aldo Caponi) and Trentadue aka Thirty-Two (Luigi Motefiori) - make a run for it. There is a gunfight with the police and a couple of officers are shot. The police are forced to tread carefully when the three fugitives take two female hostages. One of the women is brutally murdered by Blade who stabs her in the throat. They get in the surviving woman's car, leaving the police stunned at what has taken place. They don't get far before they realise the police know what vehicle they are travelling in, so they decide to change their mode of transport once again.

The next car happens to be driven by Riccardo (Riccardo Cuciolla), a man taking his sick son to hospital. This sets off a heated debate amongst them all. They all have a sense of mistrust - in the case of the hostages, this stems from

fear about what is going to happen to them, especially Riccardo who is desperate to get medical attention for his son. The criminals' mistrust comes from knowing that the hostages will try to escape and betray them to the police the first chance they get. There begins a tense cat-and-mouse game between the five individuals (six, if you include the child). The suspense is heightened by the fact that Blade and Thirty-Two are dangerously psychotic. The third crook Doc is also clearly dangerous, but seems to be the calm, relatively sane leader of the trio.

The bulk of the story from this point forth is set in the confined space of the car. I think it prudent to cut short my synopsis here, as I really don't want to spoil the film for anyone who has not yet seen it.

Suffice to say, nearly every scene is tense for one reason or another. The fugitives are constantly fearful of running into the police, even though they changed cars and seem to have thrown them off the scent. They use the car radio to listen to bulletins, learning from this that the police are close to discovering the identity of the dead getaway driver. Doc carries the stolen money, but it starts to dwindle as they have to use it from time to time, like getting through a toll gate or paying for petrol. In a tense moment, Riccardo crashes into the back of a car in a traffic jam (it is open to interpretation whether he does this deliberately). The result is an altercation between the two drivers, and Doc has to step in and offer the other driver money. It ends up costing him 60,000 of the stolen lire to sort the problem out.

The sick child shows signs of waking and Riccardo grows concerned. He asks if they can pull over to give him medication. He wants to keep the child docile, so he doesn't realise what's going on and become distressed. Maria also says she needs to pee. This leads to the film's most unsettling scene, during which she stupidly makes a run for it and is pursued by Blade and Thirty-Two. She reaches a farmhouse but there is nobody at home and she is soon recaptured. Thirty-Two points out she hasn't been to the toilet and they proceed to humiliate her by making her remove her panties and trousers, watching while she urinates and soils her clothing. This sounds disgusting but is fairly tame if compared with similar scenes from contemporary films like *Straw Dogs* (1971) and *Last House on the Left* (1972). Nevertheless, it is still an uncomfortable and tense moment. When they get back to the car, the incident seems to have triggered something in Blade and Thirty-Two, and they continue to humiliate Maria. Around this point, Doc seems to start losing control of the situation for the first time, and it takes Riccardo refusing to drive to defuse things.

They make a pit-stop for food and drink, and Riccardo is seen by a woman who knows him. He manages to get rid of her by saying he is on a trip with friends (he is accompanied by Thirty-Two anyway, so cannot tip her off about their predicament).

A little while later, the car is dangerously close to running out of fuel and they stop for petrol where they come across a very unhelpful attendant. He relents on hearing they have a sick child, but a woman suddenly appears and forces herself into the car, saying she needs a lift. She is very talkative and sets them all on edge. She asks what is wrong with the child as she is a nurse, and soon becomes suspicious. Blade puts an end to her with a well aimed knife to the throat. Soon after, they reach their destination where Riccardo and Maria fear for their lives.

The climax erupts in violence and there is a final twist which pretty much turns the film on its head. However, it works quite effectively and is consistent with the nasty and brutal tone throughout.

I rewatched *Rabid Dogs* specifically to write this article. It had been a while since I last saw it, but it still managed to surprise me, which is a strong indication of how effective and unpredictable it is.

Rabid Dogs is not perfect. It has a few flaws in its story, not least the ineffectiveness of the police who seem to lose all track of the villains by the end... and I found it unconvincing how so few of the people they come across during the journey seem able to put two and two together. However, it maintains tension for the duration and is enhanced by the strong performances from the small cast.

Cucciolla as Riccardo (a role originally meant for Al Lettieri, and also rumoured to be offered to Ernest Borgnine and Martin Balsam) is fine in the role. Lander as Maria, the woman in the wrong place at the wrong time, gives a good performance also. Poli's Dettore (aka Doc, the gang leader) seems calm and collected at first, well in control, but loses it towards the end and takes drastic action. This too is a solid performance. Caponi, playing Bisturi (aka Blade), gives an unsettling, psychotic turn. He may seem the calmer of the two psychos, but he's still prepared to kill at the blink of an eye. Montefiori plays Thirty-Two (Maria finds out why he has that nickname) and is clearly the most unbalanced of the odious trio, showing a particularly nasty side when he is drunk. He is probably the most familiar cast member, especially under his regular screen name George Eastman. He appeared in many films, including spaghetti westerns, crime, action, science fiction and horror entries, often of the exploitative variety. He gives a typically convincing performance here.

Lamberto Bava (Mario's son) made some small adjustments to the film years later, adding musical accompaniments to the soundtrack and tinkering with certain sequences for the 2002 American edit re-titled *Kidnapped*. But the original cut is the one I would advise you to see - it's Mario Bava's vision, and by far the best version there is.

David Michael Brown examines how The Who's Quadrophenia resurrected the band and inspired a new generation.

In 1979, The Who inadvertently found themselves at the forefront of a youth revolution. The 'Oribble 'Oo (Pete Townshend's band of mod-hipsters-turned-stadium-filling-rock-Gods) were on the verge of collapse. Their talismanic drummer Keith Moon was a shadow of his lunatic self and his performances and behaviour were becoming increasingly erratic. Townshend was worried that the young upstarts who had once screamed "hope I die before I get old" were now threatening to become irrelevant. The Who had joined Pink Floyd and Led Zeppelin *et al* as much-derided rock dinosaurs, scorned and spat at by the burgeoning anti-social punk movement who were disillusioned with the life that lay ahead of them under Margaret Thatcher.

The band found salvation in Franc Roddam's *Quadrophenia*, based on their 1973 heady concept album of the same name. By looking to the past and capturing that lightning-in-a-bottle moment from the '60s, the disenfranchised 'yoof' of the late '70s saw the life they wanted. *Quadrophenia* lit the torch paper of youth rebellion. An album written almost a decade earlier became the soundtrack of their lives.

"In 1972 I was twenty-eight, writing about London and Brighton in 1963 and 1964 when the band was just starting," explained Townshend, talking to Irish website 'Entertainment' while the band were touring the *Quadrophenia* album in its entirety in 2013. "I was still young enough to remember how it felt to be sixteen or seventeen and at war with my parents, bosses and authority. I could still remember that feeling of struggling to fit in, something that happened to me when I was even younger, around fourteen, and everyone around me seemed to have got their lives on track. This is such a universal experience for young people that it has echoed."

The film was a catalyst for the

new mod movement that brought the '70s to a close. The kids were ditching leather jackets, mohawks and the Sex Pistols for sharp suits, scooters, parkas and Northern Soul. The film kicked-started acting careers, inspired musicians and created fashions. From The Jam through Britpop to Oasis, the influence is tangible throughout British pop culture.

It wasn't the first time Pete Townshend's music had been adapted for the big screen. 1975 had seen director/agitator/provocateur *par excellence* Ken Russell deliver *Tommy*, a delightfully over-the-top cinematic vision of The Who's beloved rock opera about a deaf, dumb and blind boy who played a mean pinball. With typically garish visuals, a cast boasting rock royalty including The Who's frontman Roger Daltrey, Eric Clapton, Tina Turner and Elton John, plus crazed turns from Ann Margret and Oliver Reed and a killer soundtrack, *Tommy* delivered on its promise to assault the senses.

Quadrophenia was the antithesis of Russell's eye-popping candy-coloured phantasmagoria. With a no-name cast full of vim and vigour - including Phil Daniels, Leslie Ash, Ray Winstone and Sting - this gritty kitchen sink drama's dingy aesthetic captures the drab beauty of a London now long lost to regentrification. As a visual accompaniment to Townshend's masterpiece, it is perfect despite being shot years after the album was released. It's easy to see why it was such a success for Roddam, artistically if not at the box office.

It was the big-screen debut feature for the British director. Riding *Quadrophenia*'s eventual wave of success, he went on to direct *The Lords of Discipline* (1983), *The Bride* (1985) - again working with Sting and Phil Daniels - *War Party* (1988) and *K2* (1991). He also joined the likes of Jean-Luc Goddard, Nicolas Roeg, Robert Altman and Ken Russell to direct a segment of the opera anthology *Aria* in 1987.

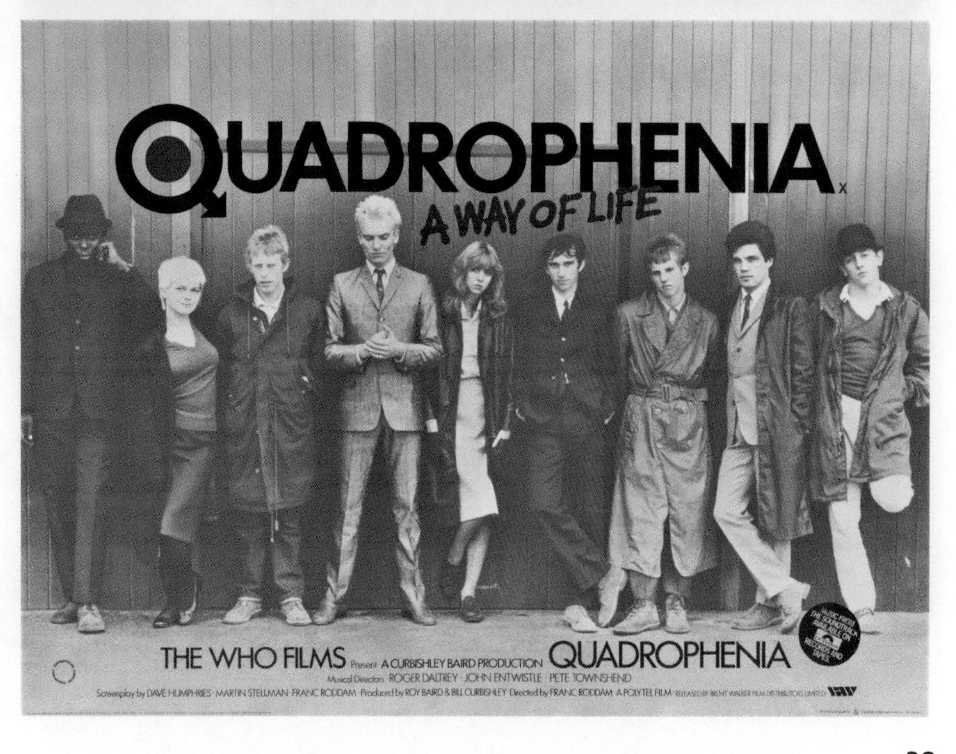

When Roddam first met Pete Townshend, The Who's chief songwriter presented him with tapes of orchestral arrangements of the score that he had produced. After his experiences with Russell on *Tommy*, Townshend assumed Roddam would also be taking the rock opera approach. The director explained he wanted to do the complete opposite and make it much more realistic in tone and style. The music from the album would still be prominent and important on the soundtrack, but he would also use songs from the era.

Both the film and the album tell the story of troubled teen Jimmy the Mod. Simplifying Townshend's complex examination of a fractured personality, the name 'Quadrophenia' - a play on 'schizophrenia' - references the four sides of Jimmy's split-personality. Townshend wrote four themes, each representing a member of the band - *Bell Boy* (Keith Moon), *Is It Me?* (John Entwistle), *Helpless Dancer* (Roger Daltrey) and *Love Reign O'er Me* (Townshend). Instead of a song-for-song recreation of the album, Roddam streamlined the narrative, focusing on the thrill and exuberance of being young.

Disillusioned Jimmy Cooper is played by Phil Daniels, ironically in a role that the Sex Pistols' frontman John Lydon aka Johnny Rotten screen-tested for (no-one would insure the film with him in it!) Living with his parents, in a dead-end job, Jimmy lives for the weekends when he can get suited and booted, pop amphetamines, speed around town on his scooter and fight rockers. These kids are no longer slaves to their parents. They are cashed-up, selfish upstarts who want to spend it all on themselves. Jimmy's mates include Steph (Leslie Ash), Chalky (Phil Davis), Dave (Mark Wingett) and Monkey (Toyah Wilcox). A young Ray Winstone also makes an appearance as Jimmy's old rocker friend Kevin, while Michael Elphick plays Jimmy's put-upon father and Timothy Spall makes an early appearance as a projectionist.

For British mods or rockers in the '60s, all roads led to Brighton. Jimmy and his mod mates arrive on a euphoric scooter-driven wave of excitement. This is when we meet Sting dancing to Booker T. and the MG's *Green Onions*. Then on the brink of global stardom thanks to the success of *Roxanne*, the Police frontman plays über mod Ace Face.

The teen factions clash on the beaches and run riot through the streets of the seaside town. The police intercept and Jimmy is picked up, and along with Ace is charged and taken to court. When he leaves Brighton, however, his life falls apart. He loses his job, his girl and his mind and in the iconic ambiguous final shot, he drives a scooter over Beachy Head and it crashes down onto the pebbly beach. In one act of defiance, Jimmy has left that part of his life behind him. He has grown up.

Daniels was working on the sequel to *Zulu* in South Africa when he was given the news. "I heard about the film on the telephone when I was in a mud hut in Africa with Bob Hoskins filming *Zulu Dawn*. I came back to audition and got a screen test and, all of a sudden, I was standing next to Pete Townshend with the biggest smile on my face, wearing a shirt with Vespa on it!"

When the young actors were cast, they were sent to "mod school". As Sting recounted to the 'New York

Times': "We'd go out with some actual London mods from the era, drinking with them, and they showed us some dance moves."

Playing Monkey, the young mod with eyes for Jimmy, Toyah Wilcox (who would go on to have a successful punk pop career after the success of *It's a Mystery*) recalled the preparation that was expected from the director. She told Ross Hemsworth on Net Talk UK Radio: "Franc wanted us to meet original mods and rockers. He wanted us to experiment with the drugs they took back then. He wanted us to know what commitment that generation made to being a mod. So, I mean the red hair came off, white hair went in its place. I had to kind of disown punk for a while which made me very uncomfortable coz I liked being a punk rocker."

Filming began on location in Brighton with 2,000 extras. The seaside town on the south coast had become the mecca for pent-up teenage rage in the '60s and *Quadrophenia* recreates this blot on the historical landscape with a panicked authenticity. The recreations of the beachfront clashes are brutal. Shopfronts are smashed as both sides are hounded and chased through the streets of Brighton by the police. Roddam's pre-production mod boot-camp ensured the brawls had the requisite gravitas. The relationships between the friends are tangible, especially a brief dalliance in an alley between Jimmy and Steph while they hide away from the police. The scene of their passionate tryst has since been renamed Quadrophenia Alley.

Despite the chaos depicted on screen, Gary Shail (who played mod Spider) recalls nothing of the sort behind the camera while filming the clashes between the mods and the rockers. He told '*suityourselfmodernists.com*': "The riot scenes were planned like a military operation, and I think it's a testament to the direction and planning that no-one, apart from a few cuts and bruises, got seriously hurt! We had no idea where the cameras were, or what they were filming at any point, so when we heard the word 'ACTION' we just all steamed in. The look of surprise and indignation on my face when I get attacked by two rockers on the beach is real, because I didn't know that they were going to do it."

On the rockers' side John Blundell, who would work again with Winstone in *Scum* the same year, played the gang leader. The actor had fond memories of the Brighton shoot, despite being involved in a multi-bike pile-up while shooting the scene when the rockers chase mod Chalky off the road. He told '*modsofyourgeneration.com*': "I spent three weeks in Brighton on the set. One of my fondest memories is that the whole cast stayed in the same hotel, and you could come down in the morning for breakfast, and hear the then-unknown Sting playing the piano, and Phil Daniels playing guitar, along with Toyah jamming, and at that time, being so young, just taking it all for granted."

After Brighton, the crew headed to London, where filming

centred around The Who's old stomping ground of West London. Scenes were shot at Shepherd's Bush Market, Goldhawk Road, Notting Hill, Queensway, Willesden and Wembley. The locations add grit and authenticity to proceedings. The scene in the pie shop where Jimmy goes for a bite of pie and mash ("pile the liquor on mate") and meets up with Kevin after their bath house encounter was shot inside the famous A. Cooke's Pie & Mash shop at 48 Goldhawk Road. The Who began their career performing their early gigs, playing as The Detours as far back as 1962, at the Goldhawk Social Club just down the road.

Quadrophenia was the second film released by The Who Films Ltd., a company set up by the band, their manager Bill Curbishley, and Roy Baird. The first release was *The Kids Are Alright*, a compilation of then little seen clips, TV interviews and live performances that director Jeff Stein saw as "a hair-raising rollercoaster ride" but ended up being a tribute to the band's late great drummer Keith Moon who died on 7th September 1978. He passed a week after he had seen a rough cut of the film and, in his honour, the band did not cut any footage from that moment. Performances captured included the band's set at Woodstock, the Monterey Pop Festival and their explosive performance of *My Generation* on *The Smothers Brothers Comedy Hour* when Moon packed his bass drum with dynamite. The blast shook the studio and set light to guitarist Townshend's hair, deafening him in the process. Realising they didn't have high quality footage of some of their most famous numbers, the band also recorded two songs, *Won't Get Fooled Again* and *Baba O'Reilly*, in front of a live audience at London's Shepperton Studios which turned out to be their last ever performance with their beloved drummer. The perfect tribute to "Moon the Loon".

Interviewed at the time of *Quadrophenia*'s release, Townshend said: "Somebody suggested putting 'This film is dedicated to the memory of Keith Moon' on *Quadrophenia*, and I said: 'you don't need it. You don't need to say it. *Quadrophenia* is Keith Moon.' They'd make a tombstone out of it. It should definitely not seem to be a tombstone for Keith, and God forbid, it turns out to be a tombstone for The Who."

The third and final film released by The Who Films was the prison break biopic *McVicar* based on the non-fiction book 'McVicar by Himself' by John McVicar. Roger Daltrey took on the role of McVicar, a hardened criminal and bank robber who was thrown in prison but escaped to the sounds of Daltrey's guttural scream and Jeff Wayne's panpipes. A foul-mouthed cockney knees-up also starring Adam Faith, Billy Murray, Brian Hall and Steven Berkoff, *McVicar* once again proves Daltrey is a talented and muscular performer, equally at home punching out a fellow con or spinning his microphone above his head in front of a stadium full of screaming fans.

Moon had passed away as *Quadrophenia* went into pre-production, briefly sending the film into chaos. The drummer had been battling an alcohol addiction for some time, and finally overdosed on heminevrin tablets, which he had been prescribed to help deal with the symptoms of acute withdrawal. Roddam recalled an early meeting with the band and their manager Curbishley. Moon was obviously a shadow of his former self, but he never lost that wicked sense of humour. He told Roddam: "I've got a great idea. Why don't we direct this movie together?" Roddam, however, was quick with his reply: "I've got a great idea. Why don't you let me drum on the next Who album?"

While the band had cameoed in *Tommy* (playing Elton John's backing band during *Pinball Wizard*), they did not appear directly in *Quadrophenia*. There are, however, several references to them throughout, including footage of them performing *Anyway, Anyhow, Anywhere* on the TV show *Ready Steady Go!*, a 'Maximum R&B' poster on Jimmy's bedroom wall, and a raucous party scene during which Jimmy puts on *My Generation* (the anachronistic sleeve of which is a repackaged Who album that was not available at the time).

They did, however, remix the old album for the soundtrack... or John Entwistle did. The bassist, nicknamed the Oz, remixed ten of the seventeen tracks from the original 1973 rock opera that appear in the film in some form. The most obvious sonic tampering is heard on the loud brash opening track *The Real Me* which was given a thunderous new bass track. Daltrey's vocals are pushed to the fore and the song was given a more definite ending. Most of the tracks are also edited to be slightly shorter. The soundtrack also includes three tracks by The Who that did not appear on the album - *Four Faces* (an outtake from the original album sessions), *Get Out and Stay Out* and *Joker James*. Moon's replacement Kenney Jones, formerly of the Small Faces, played on the last two. When the soundtrack was released, it also included some of the era-defining tunes that Jimmy and his mod mates would listen to.

Despite the band's huge fanbase, *Quadrophenia* was only a moderate success at the box office in the UK. What it did do, however, was affect everyone who saw it. The young working-class everyman struck a power chord with young cinemagoers. For Townshend, it was that acceptance and the audience response that was important to him. He explained to 'Clash Music': "I had experienced success with the *Tommy* film, and it wasn't all that enjoyable. I remember just hoping *Quadrophenia* would be a good film once it emerged. I believed it was. I remember Roy Baird, one of the producers, saying that he thought it was a 'good little British film.' I realized a few days later that he meant this as a massive compliment to the makers of the movie."

Let's Be Franc...

Adapting any work of art for the silver screen is a fraught business. From placating the original creator on an artistic level to appeasing the rabid fanbase, there are a lot of people to please. When director Franc Roddam made his feature directing debut in 1979 with *Quadrophenia* (an adaptation of one of The Who's most beloved albums), he was taking on rock royalty. David Michael Brown spoke to the director about working with Pete Townshend, choreographing a riot in Brighton, and casting Sting.

DMB: *Quadrophenia* still resonates with new generations. What is it about the film that gives it this longevity?

FR: It's a combination of many things. Of course, it's the original music by Pete Townshend and his original concept… I think it still plays really well; the quality of acting from Phil Daniels and the other guys (I think Phil Daniels is terrific in the film). And I think it's the authenticity of the piece. The emotions are genuine. The other thing about it is that 99% of movies that were out when I was making my movie were all about winning, all about being the best. Young people are very insecure. They have freedom without experience. *Quadrophenia* is about teenage angst and is about failing. Jimmy loses his job, his girlfriend and his family. He contemplates suicide. This is about things not working out.

DMB: So, it's like real life…

FR: Exactly, it's what a lot of people go through. So many young people appreciate the fact. He's a fuck-up, basically. [*Laughs*]

DMB: How did you get involved with the film? How did a first-time director land such a high-profile project?

FR: I'd directed a drama on television called *Dummy*. It won the RAI drama prize at Prix Italia that year. It got a lot of attention and a lot of people watched it. I think 14 million people watched the show. Every other adult in the country had seen it. You'd go out anywhere and people would be talking about it. It was because of that. The Who's management at the time were looking to make the film and were looking for a director. They asked David Puttnam, and he suggested me. Then they asked Alan Parker, and he suggested me. So, the guys called me up and I had a meeting. They were just fantastic. They had the money from the record company but didn't have a script at all. They more-or-less said: "we have to go now. Will you do this?" I leapt at the chance! I brought in a writer friend of mine and we did the first draft. And then I got in another writer to work on the second draft with me. Whilst we were writing, we went into pre-production. It happened really quickly. I got hired in June and I was shooting at the end of September.

DMB: *Quadrophenia* featured a largely unknown cast. Was that a deliberate decision on your part?

FR: Very much so. On all these occasions, producers will thrust young actors on you and think they will make a difference to the box office. I argued very strongly that these guys were meant to be 18 years old. Even if we used 20 or 21 year-olds, they hadn't done anything significant to make an impression on a worldwide audience. I was determined to just go for the best people. I hustled them into believing this was the best route. This says something about the film's producers, and Roy Baird and Bill Curbishley (who was the band's manager). They went along with the decision. As did The Who, by the way. Pete Townshend was fantastic, very gracious about the whole process.

DMB: What involvement did the members of The Who have with the film? Were they hands on?

FR: No, not at all. What was great about them, especially Pete (because it was his baby), was that they understood the process. He realised that *he* was providing the music, but *I* was making the film. We had some discussions about the way the film would look and the direction it was going to take. I didn't want a rock opera. I wanted a realistic movie. I was going to make a street movie. I wanted to use rock 'n' roll and I wanted loud guitars. And it couldn't be just The Who music because that wouldn't be realistic. That was the most important discussion I had with The Who and certainly with Pete. He was very easy. Roger was talking about style, so that was good. The one I worked with the most was John Entwistle on music because we did all the post-production together. We spent a few months together. Unfortunately, Keith [Moon] had died a few weeks before we shot the film. When I did meet him, he was very funny and very cheeky. He was a real handful. So, my experience working with The Who was great.

DMB: How did you find Phil Daniels? (He is extraordinary in the film).

FR: I had a very good casting director called Patsy Pollack. Her job was to lay a lot of people in front of me. She found them from all over the place. Phil came from a blue-collar, part-time acting school for kids in North London called the Anna Scher Theatre School. I knew Ken Loach had got people from there and he's a hero of mine. Phil was a graduate but a lot of kids in my films come from there. It's an improvisational school. We hadn't even written the script at this stage, so I was getting the kids to improvise to get ideas. What was clear was that Phil, who had done some acting at this stage, was pretty fantastic. I saw him early in the process, but he had just come back from South Africa shooting *Zulu Dawn*. He had a green tongue; he was sick. I didn't want to go anywhere near him, let alone have him in the movie! I went on and saw another 2000 people including people like Johnny Rotten, but I saw Phil again when he was healthy, and I realised he was the best by far.

DMB: Can you talk about the casting of Sting?

FR: He was in The Police at that point, but they hadn't released an album. I think he was a part-time janitor at the time. I wanted whoever who played the Ace Face to look different from everyone else. Then Sting walked into the room. He was older than the other actors, which helped. It gave him gravitas. He looked like a Nazi! [*Laughs*]

DMB: Can you talk about shooting the riot scenes in Brighton? Watching them now, they are huge. There are so many extras! In terms of logistics, how complicated was the whole sequence to shoot?

FR: I discovered early on that I am very good with big scenes. I think that comes from my love of early cinema. For me it was easy but for the people standing behind me, it was tough. One of the hardest things was getting all the locations in Brighton. When we had them all, shooting the riots was terrific fun. What I realised was every time

we started shooting, we got free extras because the crowds started watching and I just integrated them into my movie. For the riot, I did a street plan and then tackled it like I was planning an attack. We showed the plans to the police, and they were rather impressed.

DMB: I'm sure no matter how organised you were, there were a few injuries along the way.

FR: You know what? It wasn't too bad. There is a scene on the beach where there are 500 people fighting, hundreds of extras watching, and 14 camera moves that take place during that process, action and stunts being called in. There were horses charging. It was really chaotic. We did the first take, the weather was perfect and the extras were watching. It was fantastic. Then one of the assistants came up to me and said: "did you see that policeman?" Now, they were the only professional extras on set. The rest were real mods or rockers. The policemen buggered it up. One had his helmet on backwards and the other was laughing. I thought, shit, we've got to do this again! We set up the shot, and I was just about to shout action when I ran over to this group of mods who had joined the film from Manchester and said to them: "these policemen are fucking it up. Go for them for real this time." Suddenly these policemen were fighting for their lives and that is why it looks so good. I probably wouldn't get away with that now. [*Laughs*] It was the energy of all the young actors that made the scenes so believable.

DMB: What was the response to the film when it was first released?

FR: The mods were so on side. The film is set in he '60s and we were filming in 1977 and 1978. Punk was in full flow, but there were mod clubs all over Britain. They all came down to be in the movie and they stayed with us for the whole Brighton shoot. We integrated and used them on the film, so they loved it. The people I got the most grief from were mod tailors. I lived just off Portobello Road. There's a mod tailor around the corner from me and he has a photo of *Quadrophenia* in his window. And he goes: "mods they ain't!" He was flying the flag for mod fashion, saying I got it wrong! [*Laughs*] He's had that in the window for 30 years! Joking aside, the mods embraced the movie. Mods around the world call *Quadrophenia* their bible. It's amazing, the lives the film has touched. I had a taxi driver in New York once who said he had seen it 200 times! He told me the film had saved his life. It's amazing that our little movie could do that.

The editors of 'Cinema of the '70s' wish to extend their thanks to Franc Roddam for his time, and David Michael Brown for conducting the interview. David's in-depth article on the film itself, can be found on page 38.

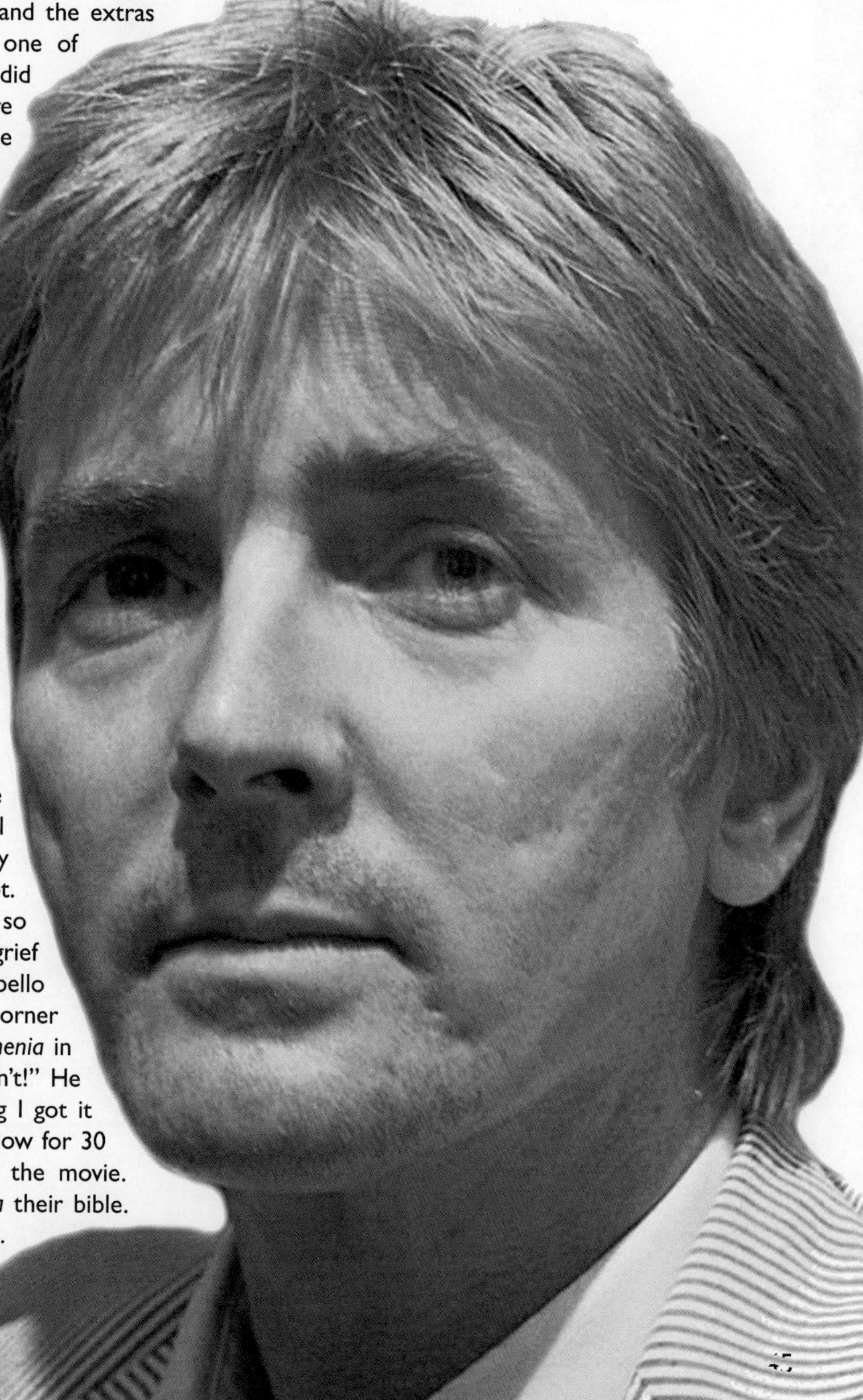

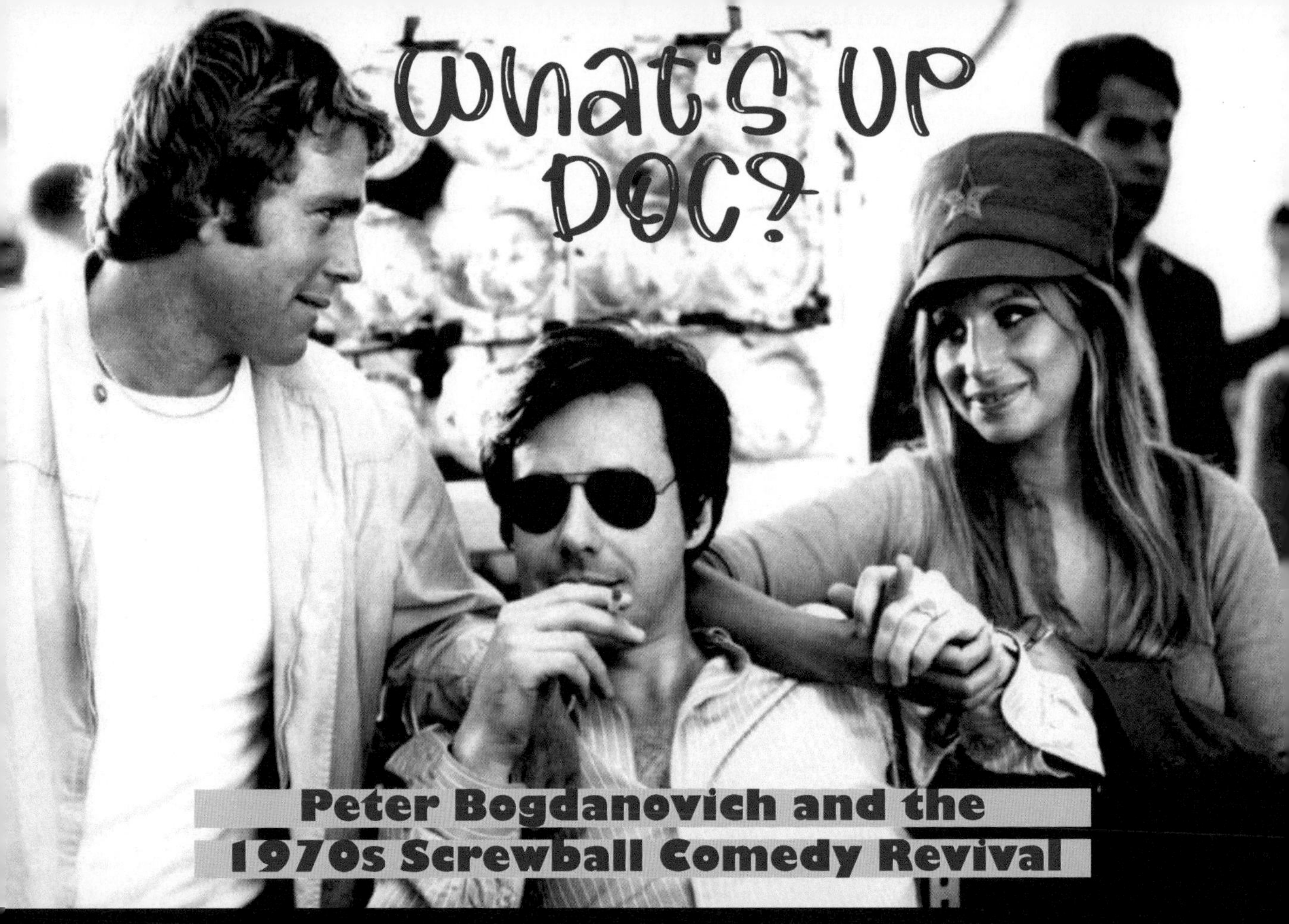

What's Up Doc?

Peter Bogdanovich and the 1970s Screwball Comedy Revival

Brian J. Robb explores the impact of director Peter Bogdanovich, and stars Barbra Streisand and Ryan O'Neal, on the revival of screwball comedy movies in the '70s.

Just as the classic Hollywood studio system went into decline as the '60s transitioned into the '70s, so Hollywood set about reviving an old genre that had long lain dormant: the screwball comedy. As the production line studio system gave way to the rise of the independents, several New Hollywood filmmakers looked to the past for their inspiration. Prime among them was Peter Bogdanovich. Many of his early films examined the past, especially through film. *Targets* (1968), for example, featured Boris Karloff as an aging horror star confronting the real-world horror of a mass shooter, climaxing at a drive-in movie theatre where real life gets confused with 'reel' life. His multiple award-winning *The Last Picture Show* (1971) was a coming-of-age drama steeped in cinematic nostalgia for the '50s, as the closure of a smalltown Texan movie theatre signifies the end of an era. Depression-set con artist comedy *Paper Moon* (1973) and early-cinema drama *Nickelodeon* (1976) both starred Ryan O'Neal, who had first worked with Bogdanovich on *What's Up Doc?* (1972), the film that gave rise to the new wave of '70s screwball comedies.

The screwball comedy originally emerged in the '30s during the Great Depression in America as a sub-genre of the romantic comedy. It continued strong through the '40s before petering out. The key to screwball was the way it both satirised traditional romantic comedy and played with gender roles, often questioning the masculinity of the central male character while presenting the main female as a dominant, capable or even scheming figure. The 'battle of the sexes' presented in screwball often became physical, offering opportunities for slapstick and comedy violence. The verbal repartee came fast and loose, with characters often talking over each other (a prime example being Howard Hawks' *His Girl Friday*, 1940). The standard aspects of romance - from meeting through seduction to marriage - were up for grabs, with class criticism thrown in for good measure. The screwball comedy was a response to the Hays censorship code that brought an end to 'pre-code cinema', the raunchy era of anything goes comedy that was shut down in 1934.

The boundaries of the original screwball era are debatable, with some scholars stretching the genre from the '20s to the '50s, but the core titles emerged between the early '30s and the early '40s. The original model screwball comedy is usually cited as Frank Capra's *It Happened One Night* (1934), starring Clark Gable and

Claudette Colbert. A series of screwball stars quickly emerged, including Cary Grant, Katharine Hepburn, Carole Lombard, William Powell, Rosalind Russell, Irene Dunne, Barbara Stanwyck and Joel McCrea. The *Thin Man* series, which kicked off in 1934, starred Powell and Myrna Loy as Nick and Nora Charles, casual crime investigators who were more interested in where their next cocktail was coming from than whodunnit. *My Man Godfrey* (1936) foregrounded the class critique as Powell's tramp is hired by Lombard's spoiled society dame to become her butler, only for romance to blossom. *The Awful Truth* (1937) spoofed divorce, with a separating couple - Irene Dunne and Cary Grant - interfering in each other's subsequent love lives. The central stars of the genre, though, were Grant and Hepburn. Across three films - *Bringing Up Baby* (1938), *Holiday* (1938) and *The Philadelphia Story* (1940, with James Stewart) - they defined the genre. Late entries included Preston Sturges' *The Lady Eve* (1941, with Stanwyck) and *The Palm Beach Story* (1942, with McCrea).

Back to the Future

It was Peter Bogdanovich and his star Ryan O'Neal who were largely responsible for the revival of the form in the '70s with *What's Up Doc?* The impetus for the movie came from female lead Barbra Streisand, who'd made her mark on Broadway in 1964 playing Fanny Brice in *Funny Girl*, which became a movie in 1968 directed by William Wyler. Streisand shared that year's Best Actress Oscar with Katharine Hepburn (who won for *The Lion in Winter* - the only time to date there has ever been a tie). Movie musicals were a natural for Streisand, so she followed *Funny Girl* with *Hello, Dolly!* (1969), *On a Clear Day You Can See Forever* (1970) and *The Owl and the Pussycat* (1970). She knew, however, that in order to thrive in movies she would have to broaden her range. It was this desire that brought her into Bogdanovich's orbit after *The Last Picture Show* was nominated for eight Oscars, including Best Picture and Best Director (it won two: Best Supporting Actor for Ben Johnson and Best Supporting Actress for Cloris Leachman).

"Barbra saw *The Last Picture Show* when it was still a work print, and she loved it and wanted to work with me," recalled Bogdanovich in the 'Hollywood Reporter'. "Warners had a picture they wanted me to do, but I didn't care for the script. John Calley, who was then head of production, called me into his office and said: 'Look, Barbra really wants to work with you. If you were going to make a picture with Barbra Streisand, what kind of picture would you do?' I said: 'Oh, I don't know, kind of a screwball comedy, something like *Bringing Up Baby*: daffy girl, square professor, everything works out all right.' He said: 'Do it.'"

Bogdanovich found himself producing and directing Streisand's next picture, although no-one beyond himself knew what it would be like. Streisand was expecting a drama, something more like *The Last Picture Show* than what she ended up in. "[Screwball] wasn't her favourite kind of material," remembered Bogdanovich. "She was disappointed that we did a way-out comedy, but she was very responsive and did everything I asked her to do." Streisand claimed that working with Bogdanovich was the first time she'd been properly directed as an actress rather than just a musical theatre star making a film. "She's so good as a comedienne that it was easy for her. She knows timing; she's just really good at it. I tried to get the best of how I saw Barbara, as funny, cute and charming and kind of a wiseass at the same time." The character of itinerant Judy Maxwell as portrayed by Streisand was screwball gold in Bogdanovich's hands.

While Bogdanovich's inspiration when it came to directing was Howard Hawks, he knew that the success of his modern screwball picture would largely rely upon the script. The director turned to the writing team of David Newman and Robert Benton who'd made an impact with their screenplay for *Bonnie and Clyde* (1967), the Arthur Penn-directed film starring Warren Beatty and Faye Dunaway often cited as ground zero for the New Hollywood that emerged in the '70s of which Bogdanovich was part. "Peter said he needed it fast because he had a 'pay or play' deal with Streisand and O'Neal," Newman said. "If he didn't have a script ready to shoot by July, they were gone. So, we flew out to Los Angeles and went into these intensive sessions with Peter where we hashed out the story. Peter would talk to Howard Hawks every night, and he'd come in the next day and say: 'Howard thinks we should try such-and-such.'"

As well as Hawks, Bogdanovich regularly consulted with Streisand, outlining the story so far and soliciting her input. That got fed into the screenplay, which led to a live read-through with Streisand, O'Neal and Bogdanovich (who played all the other roles). "At the end of [that], they both committed to it," said Bogdanovich. Three weeks before filming, however, Warner's John Calley concluded the script they had was "a terrible piece of shit. I was sitting by my pool reading it on a Saturday. I wanted to blow my brains out. It was just awful." Bogdanovich's then-wife, production designer Polly Platt, agreed… but she had an idea. "I told Peter that one solution would be to reverse the roles - give Ryan the nagging part, and Barbra the irresponsible role and then it might be tolerable." Platt was also responsible for a switch of the film's location, from Chicago (which she didn't think was funny) to San Francisco (which she did).

Calley brought in Buck Henry (who co-wrote *The Graduate*, 1967, for Mike Nichols, and who was an uncredited writer on Streisand's *The Owl and the Pussycat*) to revamp the screenplay. As Bogdanovich remembered, Henry said to him: "You're going to hate me, but I don't think it's complicated enough. You need another suitcase." The director said: "So, we added the whole Top Secret suitcase which was inspired by the Pentagon Papers story. That's why we cast Michael Murphy, because he looked a bit like Daniel Ellsberg. Buck rewrote the script, which is more-or-less what we shot. We made up some of the jokes as we were planning and shooting it."

Which Case is Which?

Those suitcases are central to the chaotic plot of *What's Up, Doc?* Four individuals all check in to the same San Francisco hotel carrying identical hold-all overnight bags. The bag belonging to Ryan O'Neal's uptight musicologist Howard Bannister contains igneous rocks with a musical quality, while Streisand's Judy Maxwell has another identical bag containing her clothing and a dictionary. Adding to the mixed-up bags chaos are two others, one belonging to the mysterious Mr. Smith (Michael Murphy) carrying purloined Top Secret government papers, and the other containing valuable jewels and belonging to wealthy socialite Mrs. Van Hoskins (Mabel Albertson). Caught up in events is Bannister's baffled fiancée Eunice (Madeline Kahn), whose identity Judy has appropriated - she seems to have her eyes on Howard, too...

As the bags are swapped between jewel thieves, government agents and each of the four owners, the centrepiece of the film is a chaotic chase through the streets of San Francisco as Howard and Judy go on the run. This exhilarating sequence begins with the pair on a purloined delivery bike, only to switch to a stolen Volkswagen Beetle decorated for a wedding, which powers through Chinatown, down the famously winding Lombard Street, and - via wet cement and a massive pane of glass crossing the road - eventually tips into San Francisco Bay.

Throughout, Streisand's crazy Judy romantically pursues O'Neal's uptight Howard in the finest screwball tradition. In signing O'Neal - who had come to the film through a Streisand connection - Bogdanovich was clear that the actor needed to change his cinematic image, which had been primarily shaped by the tragic *Love Story* (1970) where he'd co-starred with Ali McGraw. Bogdanovich had seen *Love Story* and hadn't been impressed. "[I] didn't like the picture, but [I] thought he was great. I thought it would be interesting to cast him against type playing an Iowa square. I had lunch with Ryan, who in those days was very funny in life. He had a wiseass kind of thing, and he was self-deprecating and charming. I liked him. I said 'If you do this, I'm going to make fun of you. You have to shorten your hair and we will put you in a seersucker suit and glasses. You're going to be square.' He loved the idea. So, we got Ryan."

Streisand was the star, however, earning $500,000, with O'Neal on $350,000. It would be O'Neal rather than Streisand that Bogdanovich would later work with again in both *Paper Moon* and *Nickleodeon*. The rest of the '70s would see mixed fortunes for the director. He met Cybil Shepherd, leaving Platt for her, and starred her in the 1974 period drama *Daisy Miller* and the 1975 musical comedy

At Long Last Love. Those two films, along with *Nickleodeon*, were box office disappointments, taking the sheen off his *Last Picture Show* boy wonder aura. He signed up to direct *Bugsy Malone* but Universal dropped him. "I was dumb," said Bogdanovich in 1976. "I made a lot of mistakes." He ended the decade with *Saint Jack* (1979), a hit with critics but another box office failure. This oddball crime comedy starring Ben Gazzara has since been rediscovered and re-evaluated and is now something of a cult movie.

The '80s would be an even more controversial decade for Bogdanovich, not so much for his work but for his personal life off-screen. He returned to Hollywood respectability with disfigurement drama *Mask* (1985), but only after the disaster of the self-distributed romantic comedy *They All Laughed* (1981), which featured Playboy model Dorothy Stratten. Bogdanovich started a relationship with Stratten, which was short-lived as she was murdered at the age of 20 by her estranged husband Paul Snider in the summer of 1980. Bogdanovich published a memoir of his time with Stratten in 1984 entitled 'The Killing of the Unicorn'. Declaring bankruptcy as a result of *They All Laughed*, Bogdanovich married Stratten's younger sister Louise in 1988. He was 49, she was 20. In the years that followed, Bogdanovich directed a poorly received sequel to *The Last Picture Show* called *Texasville* (1990), the stage-derived *Noises Off* (1992), one of River Phoenix's last films *The Thing Called Love* (1993) and *The Cat's Meow* (2001), a return to the exploration of the legends of early Hollywood that had driven his initial filmmaking.

The Screwball Revival

What's Up, Doc? was a huge hit for Bogdanovich, Streisand and O'Neal in March 1972. Against a production budget of $4 million, it went on to make a whopping $66 million, making it the third highest US grosser of the year after *The Godfather* and *The Poseidon Adventure*. Critic John Simon called the film "a heavy-handed attempt at nostalgia", but it was popular enough to see two US re-releases, first in 1973 taking an additional $3 million at the box office, and again in 1975, where it brought in a further $6 million in takings.

Other critics rated the movie better than Simon (upon whom Bogdanovich had supposedly based the character of Hugh Simon, allowing Kenneth Mars to deliver a highly eccentric performance). Peter Travers hailed the "remarkable performances" Bogdanovich had elicited from his cast, while Rex Reed claimed that "Peter Bogdanovich puts the magic back into movies." In 'Saturday Review', Arthur Knight hailed *What's Up, Doc?* as "unflaggingly funny", while 'Variety' described it as "a total smash. The script and cast are excellent. The direction and comedy staging are outstanding."

The undoubted success of *What's Up, Doc?* provoked a revival of the screwball comedy form in the mid-'70s.

The directors behind these films had grown up in the '40s when the screwball pioneers like Howard Hawks, Frank Capra, Leo McCarey, Preston Sturges and George Cukor were at their height. Updating the screwball sensibility to the social mores and cultural concerns of the '70s came naturally. Streisand returned to the form in 1974's *For Pete's Sake*, directed by Peter Yates and co-starring Michael Sarrazin. Having incurred a debt with a failed stock market gamble, an ordinary New York housewife finds her debt passed from one corrupt individual to another. She gets caught up in prostitution, terrorism and cattle rustling while trying to keep her endeavours secret from her husband, Pete (Sarrazin). At the end of the decade, Streisand again teamed with Ryan O'Neal in *The Main Event* (1979), in which she manages and coaches young boxer Eddie 'Kid Natural' Scanlon (O'Neal) as a way of escaping a financial misfortune.

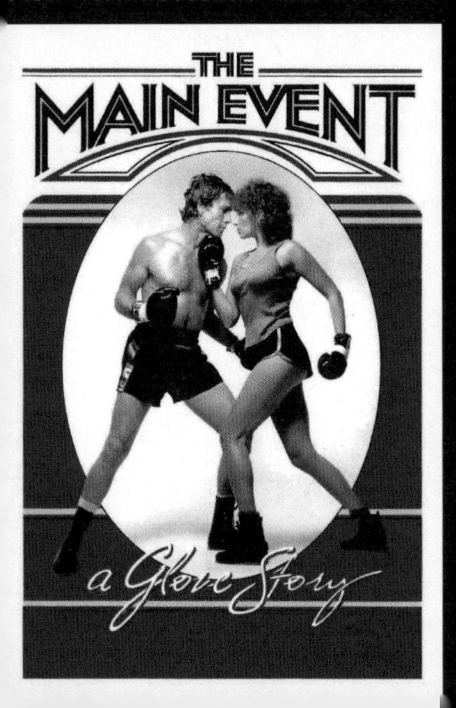

The directors of the '70s didn't just update the screwball comedy, they personalised it to make it fit with their own wider concerns. Bogdanovich consciously drew upon *Bringing Up Baby*, but his background was as a film critic and Hollywood historian, so that makes sense. For someone like John Cassavetes, coming from live television and independent cinema, his perspective on the genre was slightly different. Like *What's Up, Doc?*, *Minnie and Moskowitz* (1971) is built around an unlikely couple who, on the surface, don't appear compatible at all. Cassavetes does, however, indulge in the same cinephilia as Bogdanovich, opening with museum employee Minnie (Gena Rowlands) and her friend Florence (Elsie Ames) at a screening of *Casablanca* (1942), and afterwards comparing their romantic lives unfavourably with those of screen stars like Humphrey Bogart and Clark Gable. "Movies are a conspiracy," claims Minnie, criticising the unreal depiction of romance. She then experiences a movie-style romance when she meets parking attendant Seymour Moskowitz (Seymour Cassel), who sets out to woo her. This being a Cassavetes film, *Minnie and Moskowitz* simultaneously employs and undercuts the conventions of the screwball genre. All the elements are present - crazy characters, offbeat happenings, whimsy, slapstick and a romance that succeeds when it simply shouldn't - but they are all filtered through Cassavetes' trademark unblinking,

even painful, realism. This is screwball with real consequences.

Elaine May is a name that would more likely be connected with the screwball genre. Certainly, her *The Heartbreak Kid* (1972) plays up the genre tropes, but is in its own way just as rooted in reality as the work of Cassavetes. Written by Neil Simon, it's a black comedy of marriage and re-marriage, as so many classic screwballs comedies were. A hasty marriage between Lenny (Charles

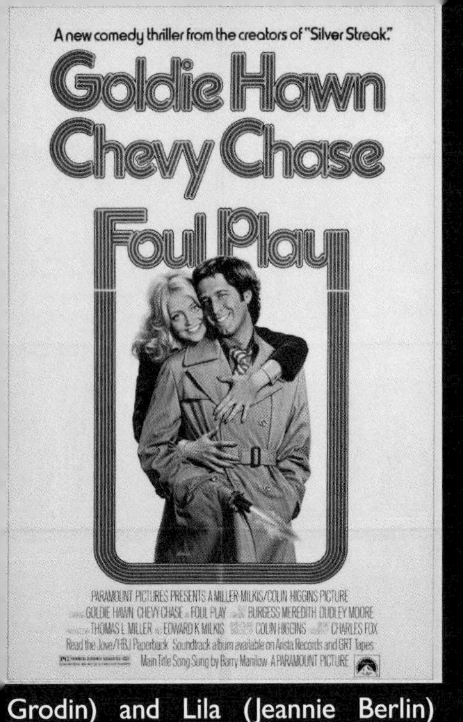

Grodin) and Lila (Jeannie Berlin) sees him abandon his bride on their honeymoon to pursue society heiress Kelly Corcoran (Cybill Shepherd). A distinctly '70s riff on *The Philadelphia Story*, *The Heartbreak Kid* explores the modern disposability of marriage, the misguided appeal of infatuation and the consequences of heart-breaking choices. It's a 'Me Generation' take on screwball that includes social climbing and Lenny's attempt to escape his Jewish background.

Throughout the decade various directors would play with aspects of the screwball comedy formula. Woody Allen tackled it through a science fiction lens with *Sleeper* (1973), while Hal Ashby revamped McCarey's *The Awful Truth* for the '70s in *Shampoo* (1975) which starred Warren Beaty, whose 1978 *Heaven Can Wait* is itself a screwball remake. Later in the decade, Goldie Hawn proved to be the heir to Claudette Colbert and Carole Lombard, as well as Streisand, appearing in *Shampoo* and leading the cast of *Foul Play* (1978) alongside Chevy Chase. The latter played up the criminal mix-up plot that Bogdanovich had drawn upon in *What's Up, Doc?*, with the hold-alls replaced with a vital roll of film hidden in a packet of cigarettes.

Mousy librarian Gloria Mundy (Hawn) finds herself attracting the attention of any number of oddballs and weirdos, all in pursuit of the roll of film she doesn't even know she has. Chase is the detective who comes to her aid (and her bed). *Foul Play* is a screwball comedy as if made by Alfred Hitchcock, with crazy characters getting caught up in an inexplicable web of intrigue (the whole things revolves around an unlikely assassination plot). It takes *What's Up, Doc?*'s mix-ups to the next level, and benefits from being set in San Francisco like the Bogdanovich film.

Even the British got in on the '70s screwball revival, with American writer-director Melvin Frank behind *A Touch of Class* (1973), in which a married American in London pursues an affair. Frank initially lined up the retired Cary Grant to star (strengthening the film's screwball connection), before offering the role to Roger Moore who instead opted to play James Bond in *Live and Let Die*. Frank ended up with George Segal and Glenda Jackson (*The Morecambe and Wise* show had brought her to Frank's attention) as the mismatched pair who find their awkward affair turning into a real relationship beyond a simple, illicit holiday romance.

The interesting question about all this is just why did the genre of screwball comedy find a new lease of life in the '70s? There are several factors - the success of Bogdanovich's *What's Up, Doc?*, the arrival of the New Hollywood movie brats who drew upon cinema's past, and the fact that auteur directors like Preston Sturges were in the process of being rediscovered as the '70s dawned. The major one, though, is that the wave of directors who dabbled in the screwball comedy in the '70s had grown up with the original '40s variety - it gave them a special connection to the genre, and they had just the right touch to update the

form for the '70s.

Screwball never really died. It simply transformed and continued into the '80s, primarily in the 'Yuppie Kidnap' movies exemplified by Jonathan Demme's *Something Wild* (1986) starring Melanie Griffith and Jeff Daniels, who essentially impersonate the kind of characters played by Streisand and O'Neal (and Hepburn and Grant before them). Goldie Hawn continued to plough the screwball furrow with the likes of *Overboard* (1987), and the Coen Brothers kicked off a stream of screwball comedies with *Raising Arizona* in 1987 (their most screwball film, though, has to be *The Hudsucker Proxy*, 1994, with Tim Robbins and Jennifer Jason Leigh). Even a mainstream comedy hit like *When Harry Met Sally...* (1989) contains screwball elements. Bogdanovich himself returned to the form with 2015's *She's Funny That Way* with Owen Wilson and Imogen Poots, but this throwback effort lacked the sure touch that had so propelled *What's Up, Doc?* and kickstarted the original '70s revival.

Seventies Screwball Comedies

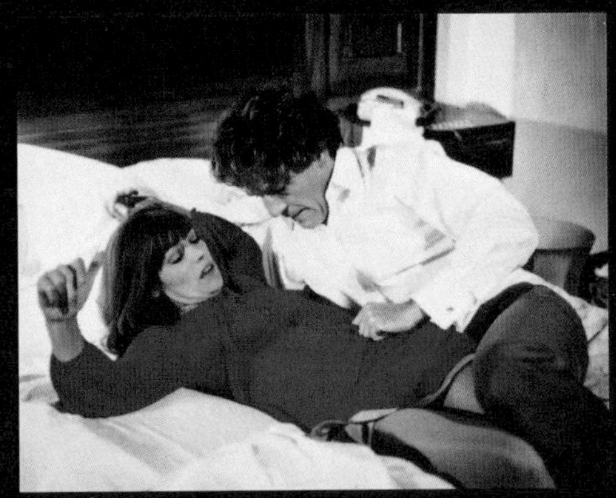

A Touch of Class (1973)

The Heartbreak Kid (1972)

For Pete's Sake (1974)

Foul Play (1978)

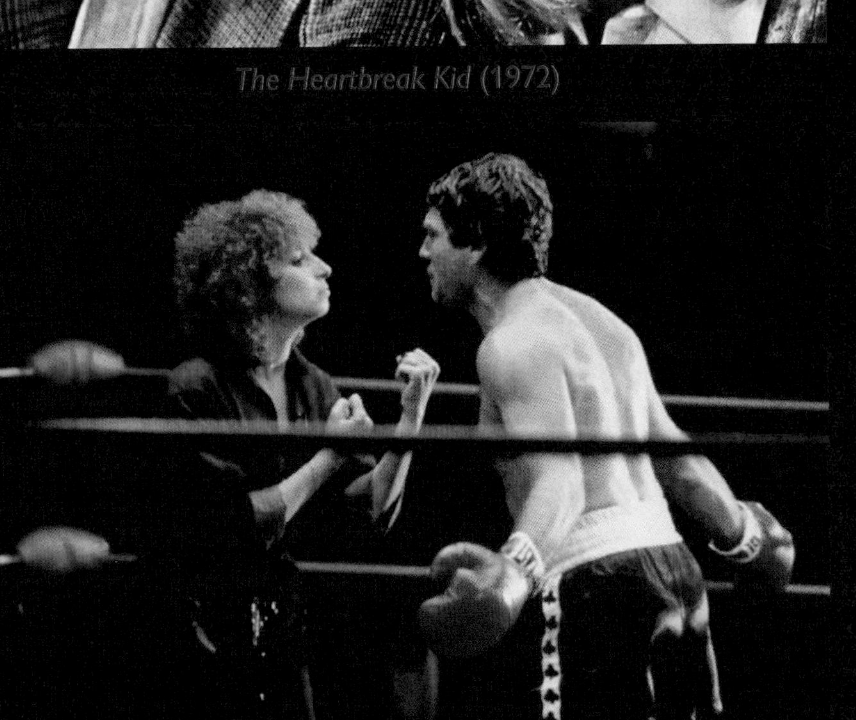

The Main Event (1979)

Minnie and Moskowitz (1971)

Throughout the '70s, Michael Caine was a busy man, appearing in over twenty films. While not all of them were box office successes or critically praised at the time, many have received better recognition retrospectively as a result of home media releases. In this article, I intend to look at two of his lesser known (but still entertaining films) from 1974. Both have certain aspects in common, perhaps coincidentally, perhaps not. A Roy Budd score on both, for example. Or the fact that Caine plays a character named John. Or that both have storylines set partially or wholly in France. They are also examples of Caine working in the Euro-thriller genre in '74.

The Black Windmill

Based on the novel 'Seven Days to a Killing' by Clive Egleton, *The Black Windmill* sees Caine as an MI6 agent Major John Tarrant, whose son is kidnapped by a mysterious gang operating under the codename "Drabble". They demand half a million pounds in diamonds for the safe return of the child and want the exchange to go down in Paris.

This a definite change of pace for Caine. His demeanor throughout is calm, almost unnervingly so. This calmness is touched upon briefly during a conversation between him and his wife. He's an MI6 agent who knows this kind of trouble well due to his job. Keeping calm under pressure is part of his training, a top priority.

Compared to more modern spy thrillers, it is quite dialogue-heavy, but occasional bursts of action help keep the story afloat. It's not gadget-heavy like the Bond films, though there is a brief sequence in a lab showing the utilisation of a briefcase which fires an explosive device. This contraption comes into play later in the story. Q from the 007 universe would certainly approve!

Supporting cast members include the always-reliable Donald Pleasence as Harper, Tarrant's superior, who is perpetually suspicious of Tarrant's activities and suspects the agent may have something to do with the kidnapping of his own son. John Vernon turns up in a typically slimy role as McKee, whose ruthless determination borders on psychotic. There's a quick blink-and-you'll-miss-it role for John Rhys-Davies as one of the kidnappers, disguised as a military policeman. Janet Suzman is effective too as Tarrant's wife, who, in most of her scenes, is encouraged to play the character as completely grief-stricken. Despite this, she still clings to the hope of her son being returned alive and is one of the few characters who trusts Tarrant throughout the whole ordeal.

The soundtrack by Roy Budd keeps the tension moving and helps in the more sombre scenes without being overbearing. It utilises a groovy undertone that really fits the vibe of the story. This was director Don Siegel's first movie in Europe at the time. A noted filmmaker, he had made *Charley Varrick* the year before, though his best-known features were probably with Clint Eastwood, most notably *Coogan's Bluff* and *Dirty Harry*. This was a big change from his American-set police dramas and it's a shame it did not pay off as a success at the box office.

Over the years, with recent DVD and Blu-ray releases, *The Black Windmill* has been re-discovered and hailed as an underrated spy film of the '70s. It has some great performances, steady action and delicate intrigue. While a little slower than the average thriller, it still packs a punch. Those who possess the required level of patience should definitely check it out.

The Destructors (aka The Marseille Contract)

DEA agent Steve Ventura (Anthony Quinn) has been trying to nail a notorious drugs baron, Jacques Brizzard (James Mason, with a slight French accent for good measure), whose gang is responsible for killing one of Ventura's undercover agents. Due to Brizzard's political connections in high places, he remains a free man and seems untouchable via official channels. So Ventura decides to go above the law by hiring an assassin. In steps Caine as John Deray, his old friend, who proceeds to infiltrate Brizzard's operation and tries to take him down.

Some might view Deray as a happier, friendlier version of Carter from *Get Carter* (1971). He enjoys his work to a degree and seems altogether more approachable. He also swears by a moral code of "No children, no women", a trope which would be used again in future films

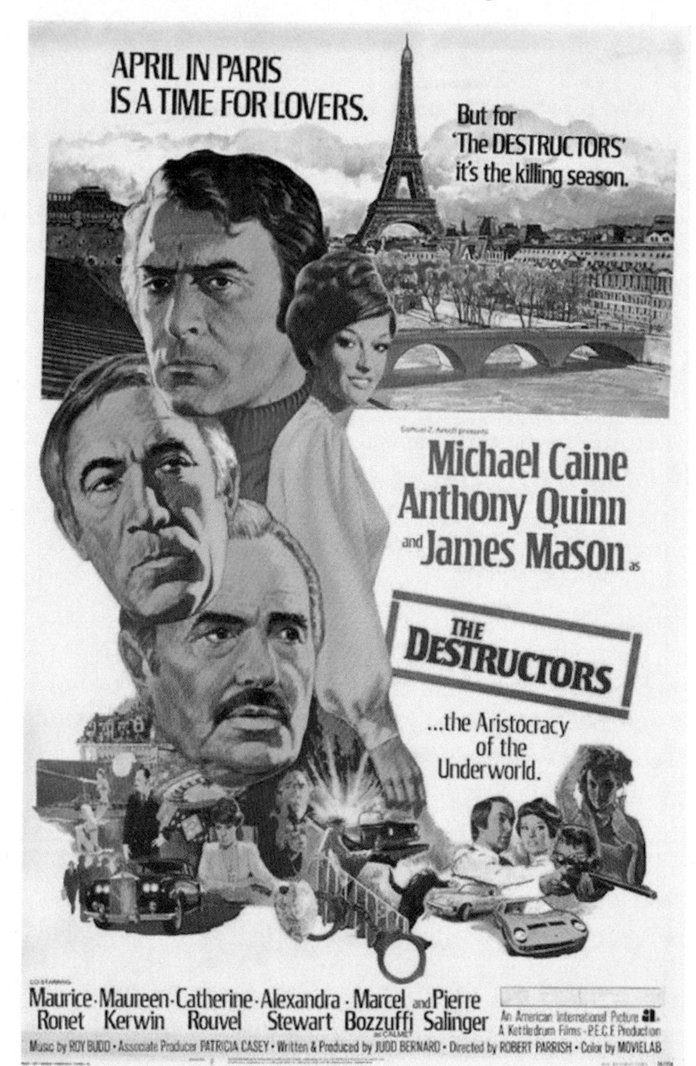

involving assassins and assassinations like *Scarface* (1983) and *Leon: The Professional* (1994). Keep in mind that while he is more jovial about his work, he is still a killer and hardly shows any hesitation. One good example is his disposal of an informant under Brizzard's orders. The scene in question takes place at the top of a tower under construction. It's quite effective - you don't expect it initially, but when he delivers the kill it's very powerfully done.

Caine and Quinn share limited screen time together, and their initial meeting hints they've been friends for quite a while. However, the script doesn't reach far into their relationship or expand upon it any further, so it all remains typically murky and mysterious.

Quinn gives a serviceable performance, quipping his way through the picture whilst avoiding multiple ambushes. Occasional side characters are brought in as informants and contacts, only to be killed off quickly and violently by Brizzard's crew. One such character is played by Marcel Bozzuffi, better known by international viewers as Pierre Nicoli from *The French Connection* (1971), the right-hand man and occasional assassin of that film's main villain Alan Charnier. Bozzuffi is not given much screen time, but his presence is always welcome. James Mason as Brizzard gives an almost regal feel to the film. His quiet demeanor seems at odds with the character's chosen lifestyle as an underworld drugs baron, but you always get a sense of the sinister side beneath.

Budd's soundtrack is rather jazzy, but also contains some typical lamenting pianos and tense, atmospheric passages which elevate the film from average to something slightly more. *The Destructors* was difficult to find for quite a while, but a recent remastered release in the United States allowed viewers the long overdue chance to finally see it.

Much like *The Black Windmill*, *The Destructors* was not a success at the box office and, after watching, you can see why. The script isn't always enlightening, and some of the performances seem lacklustre. Overall, though, it's nowhere near as bad as certain critics have implied. Caine is remarkably effective as John Deray and, once the action kicks in, you get a plethora of shootouts, betrayals and chases. Add to that the obligatory '70s twist ending, and you're looking at a pretty effective little action film.

Andy 'Location Finder General' Ellis visits the sites where the film was shot, offering pics of how it was then and how it is now.

PRESTIGE B
TO
PEPPER, A
& YARV
73 BROOK ST. L
01-499

THE OUTFIT
ARMED AND DANGEROUS!
by Julian Hobbs

If you wanted to pick the quintessential, hard-boiled '70s crime thriller for a budding young cineaste to watch as an introduction to the genre, *The Outfit* (1973) is as good a place to start as any. Its director John Flynn was a protégé of Hollywood mainstays Robert Wise and John Sturges. An undervalued craftsman whose no-nonsense style echoed that of his better-known mentors, Flynn began his career at the bottom and steadily worked his way up the ladder for a good decade before landing his first directorial gig. His directorial debut *The Sergeant* - produced under the aegis of Robert Wise - was an unusual, gay-themed drama starring Rod Steiger. It remains underappreciated and rarely screened to this day.

After this promising start, there was a setback - the box office bomb *The Jerusalem File* (1972). But afterwards, Flynn found his true métier with *The Outfit*, a bone-crunching thriller perfectly scripted by the director himself from a book of the same name by Richard Stark (the pseudonym of Donald E. Westlake). These pulpy classics featured Westlake's perennially popular character Parker, an uncompromising career criminal who made the jump from page to screen in works as diverse as Jean Luc Godard's impenetrable *Made in USA* (1966), John Boorman's existential thriller *Point Blank* (1967), the trashy *Slayground* (1983), the troubled Mel Gibson star vehicle *Payback* (1999) and *Parker* (2013) with Jason Statham, to name a few.

With their vengeance-driven plots and brutal violence, the Parker books were always going to be ideal for screen adaptation. In *Point Blank*, generally hailed as the greatest of the bunch, Lee Marvin's loose cannon crook takes on the might of the 'Corporation' (i.e. the Outfit), a monolithic crime organization that is run on corporate business lines, tapping into contemporary fears about links between the Mafia, big business and central government. Boorman's classic is much more enamored of experimental New Wave French cinema than Stark's pulp-perfect books. Later, *Payback* aped Quentin Tarantino's penchant for no-holds-barred violence and cynical black comedy in a bid to create cult movie immortality. *The Outfit* reflects the cinematic trends of the day as much as the other two while remaining the most faithful cinematic representation of the Parker universe. Having said that, what makes it truly memorable is its understated, melancholy vibe.

Earl Macklin (Robert Duvall, a force of nature) is a career criminal just coming off a short stretch for illegal arms possession. Greeted at the prison gates by his on/off squeeze Bett (Karen Black), Macklin's world is turned upside down when he learns his brother has been killed by the Mob. Worse still, his girlfriend has set him up for a hit as they spend a night together in a cheap hotel. Tipped off by Bett in the nick of time, he sends the assassin packing in typically brutal fashion before calling on his old friend Cody (Joe Don Baker at his good ol' boy best) to partner-up and take on the Outfit, who sanctioned the hit because Macklin and his gang had unwittingly knocked over one of their banks. Motivated as much by professional pride as the death of his brother, Macklin's crew start heisting more Outfit-run banks; he figures $250,000 dollars is what they owe him in loss of earnings. The three find these banks surprisingly easy pickings, at least to start with. However, they soon learn that once you've stirred the hornet's nest of organized crime, backing out isn't going to be easy… especially when you've raised the ire of Mailer (Robert Ryan), the Outfit's overlord.

Made during a time when many famous faces from film noir were still busy as jobbing actors, *The Outfit* offers a fascinating link to that late '40s/early '50s period of landmark crime thrillers and the more nihilistic universe of '70s action cinema, particularly the work of Sam Peckinpah. It is easy to spot the similarities between this and Peckinpah's *The Getaway*, though Flynn's approach is radically different in tone and style. One always knew Peckinpah's meticulous editing was building suspense for the slow-motion, montage-heavy shotgun mayhem to follow. Flynn, however, shoots in a more neutral fashion, with the violence often exploding - shockingly - at the drop of a hat, providing a visceral charge that is very much his own. A shootout at a mission, for instance, where Macklin is double crossed, quickly descends into chaos in a completely plausible way.

Flynn eschews the misogyny that was undoubtedly present in Peckinpah's work by giving his female characters a fairer crack of the whip. In Peckinpah's *The Getaway*, for instance, when McQueen's bank robber finds out MacGraw's moll has cheated on him, there is a slapping scene so unnecessarily protracted that the director of any chauvinistic Italian *polizioteschi* flick would surely have yelled cut. In *The Outfit*, Macklin quickly forgives Bett for her betrayal when he realizes torture has been used against her. In a distinctly unmacho touch, he does not even mind that she's slept with other men when he was in prison ("You did what you had to do"). Bett shows her mettle later, memorably running over two hoods when a heist goes pear-shaped. In fact, all the women here are characterised with more depth than their counterparts in the unforgivingly macho world of crime cinema. Even Sheree North's nymphomaniac wife, whose character could have existed solely for a little titillation, emerges as a fully rounded human who hits on Cody simply because she is stuck in a loveless marriage with Bill McKinney's boorish mechanic. Flynn does not expect us to sympathise with her actions, just to understand them.

If the world-weary fatalism of Macklin and Cody's career criminals reflects Peckinpah's leading men, Bloody Sam's romanticism is largely absent. That said, Flynn - like so many filmmakers - obviously admired how the great maverick revolutionised action cinema. He casts *The Wild Bunch's* Robert Ryan as the Outfit's boss, then homages it by having *Shall We Gather at The River?* sung before a shootout. He also hires Peckinpah's longtime collaborator Jerry Fielding to compose the soundtrack. Fielding provides the kind of propulsive, funky percussive vibes that were all the rage in the wake of Lalo Schifrin's game-changing work on *Bullitt* and *Dirty Harry*, nicely contrasted with a more lyrical, folksy sound for the quieter moments.

When action is the focus, it is a good idea to cast a lead actor who can say as much with a look or a gesture as a full page of dialogue. Duvall is as good as it gets from this school. A reined-in lead allows Black and Baker to strut their stuff, the latter convincingly charming, yet with no compunction about using violence if needed (he punches out a receptionist with almost shocking casualness). The carefully played relationship between the men borders on a bromance, which feeds into the almost buddy movie-like conclusion.

Black, of course, was one of the finest actresses to emerge from the New Hollywood scene and brings real depth to the show. From her rabbit-caught-in-the-headlights look early on to her steadily evolving grit in the heist game, she is uncomfortable with violence but completely trapped by circumstance. Indeed, the whole thing is exceptionally well cast, with the incomparable Timothy Carey (at his most reptilian) one of several outstanding turns from those who were active during the golden age of film noir (Elisha Cook Jr., Marie Windsor, Roy Roberts and Emile Meyer all steal scenes too).

No actor elevated that genre more than Robert Ryan. He was equally at home playing flawed heroes or deeply flawed, near-neurotic villains. That latter trait is well to the fore here, especially when Duvall's loose cannon crook meets the crime lord face to face and dares to demand a payoff. Seeing the sparks fly between two acting greats from the old and new school is a real pleasure for discerning cineastes! The deep disdain Mailer has for Macklin's *'penny ante'* operation is echoed in dealings with Carey's goon, Menner: he detests his sleazy underling yet must accept that these are the types you employ to run a profitable operation dealing in vice, corruption and violence. The slightly deluded Mailer sees himself as more of a company director (shades of *Point Blank* here) than a hood and cannot be seen bending to the will of a loose cannon stick-up artist, which, ultimately, proves to be a costly mistake. A drolly amusing but also slightly

sad touch reveals Mailer is obviously more interested in spending lavishly - and gazing lovingly - at his trophy wife (a fresh-faced Joanna Cassidy), nearly fifty years his junior, with whom he has absolutely nothing in common. Yet that weary look in his eyes tells us he knows more violence will soon be coming his way, if not from Macklin, then perhaps even his own superiors for not neutralising the gang soon enough. Tragic reality may also account for that sad look in Ryan's eyes: the great man was dying from cancer, and this marked his penultimate screen appearance.

Much credit for the look of the picture belongs to Bruce Surtees, an accomplished cinematographer best known for his long collaboration with Clint Eastwood. Favoring a deliberately drab color palette, Surtees emphasizes the depressing nature of the down-at-heel northwestern locations. Such a grim backdrop provides an authentic setting for the gritty drama. More importantly, we understand why Macklin will happily break any law to escape this world of run-down farms, dive motels and cheap diners. That said, there is a bleak beauty in this landscape too, particularly prominent in the opening sequence where Macklin's brother is cold-bloodedly murdered by two hit men (in a brutally cynical touch, one wears a priest's collar). Flynn - wisely - does not show the murder, instead cutting to the reaction of a pet Alsatian and horses bolting across a field at the sound of gunshots. It's just one of several sad, near poetic moments that generally go unnoticed by those only here for the shotgun mayhem.

Like *The Friends of Eddie Coyle* (Peter Yates' more downbeat and celebrated depiction of the underworld released the same year), there is a sense of a criminal community which exists alongside, yet completely apart from, the mainstream world. That detail emerges through some expertly played vignettes, including a smart scene with Emile Meyer, playing an enthusiastic illegal gun salesman (this business uncannily echoes De Niro's Travis Bickle buying an arsenal of guns from a travelling salesman in *Taxi Driver* three years later). Perhaps the most memorable interlude, however, comes courtesy of old reliable Richard Jaeckel, whose perfectionist hot car mechanic manages to fit a Porsche engine into a VW Beetle yet is still unhappy because he cannot engineer that authentic VW sound for it! Such attention to detail shows the care with which the film has been assembled; there is no marking time to the next shootout/punch up.

If there is one aspect that stops *The Outfit* just short of being a crime classic, it is the ending. Although tragedy does strike before the inevitable final gun battle, a more upbeat conclusion was shot late on at the studio's insistence. I don't have a problem with key characters surviving to the end credits - you like these people and certainly want to see them live - but there is something rather unconvincing, almost offhand, about the way their escape is engineered. I found that it jarred with the believability of the drama up to that point. Still, that's the only brickbat I can possibly throw *The Outfit's* way.

Three years later, Flynn cemented his reputation as a tough thriller specialist with the Vietnam vet revenge drama *Rolling Thunder*, so liked by Tarantino that he borrowed the title to name his own production company! Flynn remained an in-demand director over the next three decades, working in TV and film, often on unpretentious, decent action fare with superstars of the day like Sylvester Stallone (*Lock Up*) and Steven Seagal (*Out for Justice*). *Best Seller* (1987), brilliantly adapted by Flynn from an inventive Larry Cohen script, is a minor classic bolstered by the powerhouse acting of Brian Dennehy and James Woods, yet it barely saw the light of a projector bulb when production company Hemdale went bust. In my book, *Best Seller* and *The Outfit* stand comparison with the finest action/thriller fare around, and both deserve the deluxe Criterion Collection/Masters of Cinema treatment on Blu Ray.

Flynn sadly left us in 2007, passing away in his sleep at the age of 75. The ensuing testimonials and career retrospectives rightly singled out *The Outfit* for special praise.

THE BIGGEST BATTLE

by Jonathon Dabell

Remember when infamous horror and poliziotteschi director Umberto Lenzi made a war epic with an all-star cast? No? Don't fret - you're probably not alone. It's fair to say *The Biggest Battle* (1978) is pretty obscure and largely forgotten despite its surprising wealth of assembled talent. In front of the camera, we have the likes of Giuliano Gemma, Henry Fonda, Samantha Eggar, Stacy Keach, Helmut Berger, John Huston, Ray Lovelock, Edwige Fenech, Guy Doleman and Rik Battaglia heading an impressive cast. This appealing mix of names was what piqued my curiosity and made me want to track it down. If, like me, you end up watching one of the English language versions, you'll probably recognise the voice of Orson Welles on narration duties too.

The film goes under numerous titles, including *The Greatest Battle*, *Il grande attaco*, *Die große Offensive*, *The Great Battle*, *The Great Attack*, *Battle Force* and *The Mareth Line*. For the purpose of this article, I'll refer to it as *The Biggest Battle*, as that was the name of the version I watched.

I should be honest from the start and confess I'm not here to put forth this movie as a neglected classic. I wouldn't even describe it as a good, solid war flick which has gone under the radar for too long and needs rediscovering. I would, however, call it a curiosity piece - an example of much-loved, eclectic actors working for the unlikeliest director imaginable on a war movie far too ambitious for the modest budget. Much of it falls flat (which shouldn't surprise anyone), but there are compensations along the way and I'll discuss them in good time. There's also the fact that completists - especially those who like the director and/or any of the stars - will find more to savour than the casual viewer.

The obvious question is: which battle of World War II is the "biggest battle" mentioned in the title? Coming to the film, I was expecting it to be about the Battle of Britain, or the Battle of El Alamein; maybe the Battle of Stalingrad, or the D-Day landings, or Operation Market Garden (particularly the extraordinary fight for Arnhem Bridge). If not those, I thought it might be about the Battle of the Bulge, the Germans' final defiant counterattack against a seemingly unstoppable Allied advance in the Ardennes in the final months of WWII. As it turns out, *The Biggest Battle* covers a lengthy period of time (1936-1943 to be precise) and depicts *several* battles during its running time. The big finale takes place during the Battle of the Mareth Line (fought in Tunisia in March 1943, with the British 8th Army up against the Italo-German 1st Army). Presumably, *that* is the campaign referred to in the movie's title? I must admit I wasn't familiar with the battle and had to look it up to learn more. I take my hat off to anyone who fought in any battle in any war, but I'm not sure that what took place in Tunisia in March 1943 has ever been called the "biggest" anything before. Certain posters carried the tagline: "The Most Awesome Battle Ever Seen!" which, with respect to anyone who lost their life in the fighting, is not an accurate description of the Battle of the Mareth Line and definitely not a true summary of the movie. Italian filmmakers were never ones to let factual verisimilitude get in the way of a little exaggerated, hyperbolic marketing, that's for sure!

Events kick off in Berlin, 1936, with citizens from various countries enjoying a meal together in celebration of the end of the Olympics. Among them are German officer Major Manfred Roland (Keach), American general Harold Foster (Fonda), grizzled war correspondent Sean O'Hara (Huston) and famous German actress Annalise Hackermann (Eggar). The conversation turns to Hitler, in particular the growing international opposition to his policies and military muscle-flexing. "It'll take more than a refusal to shake the hand of an American negro [Jesse Owens] to start a war," declares General Foster. "I can assure you the Fuhrer has no intention of starting a war," agrees Roland. The guests express their desire to meet again in four years at the next Olympics, and Roland and Foster exchange gifts (each man having bought a medal for the other, engraved by coincidence with the same motto: In God We Trust).

Fast-forward six years. The story now splinters into various vignettes, some featuring the characters we've already met in the opening scene, others introducing new faces to the mix. In Los Angeles, General Foster has been recalled to active duty despite his age. His youngest son, John (Lovelock) signs up for combat in an effort to impress his father (who has always been fonder of John's older brother). In Berlin, Roland and Annalise are now married after initially meeting in that opening scene. Roland fights for his country but hates summarily executing enemies, preferring to take them prisoner where possible. We learn that Annalise has Jewish ancestry and has been hiding in a hotel throughout the war. O'Hara is in London covering the situation for the press. He desperately wants to be transferred to the North African front because he wants to "see Carthage before [he] dies." Then there's British commando, Captain Scott (Gemma), who seems to be the man-of-the-moment whenever dangerous missions are being assigned. We first see him leading an ill-fated raid on a German installation in Crete. Later, he is instructed to clear a vital minefield before daybreak so that Allied tanks can launch an attack against the German frontline. There's also the story of a reluctant French prostitute, Danielle (Fenech), forced into the sex industry to make ends meet after the death of her husband. One soldier who gives her money out of the kindness of his heart, no sex required, is Lt. Kurt Zimmer (Berger). But though he treats Danielle kindly, Zimmer is clinical and ruthlessly professional once he's in uniform. His dedication to the cause is absolute, in stark contrast with the conflicting emotions of Major Roland, and he carries out combat duties with relish.

In terms of dates and locations, the story jumps around chaotically. Close attention is required to stay abreast of where we are and who we're following at any given moment. But the various strands eventually converge, with many of the protagonists finding themselves fighting in the Battle of the Mareth Line at the climax. Not everyone is directly involved in this climactic mayhem. Fonda's character, for example, watches from afar, occasionally speaking on the radio to his son (who *is* in the thick of the action). Eggar's Jewish fugitive is captured earlier and interrogated by

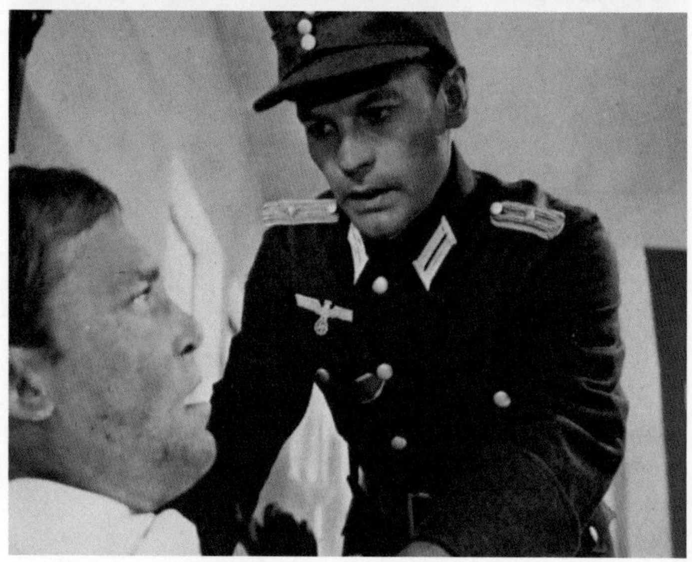

the SS, preferring suicide over giving them information. And Fenech's character learns to enjoy prostitution and the money it brings after initially loathing it. Weirdly, her story arc takes place in Le Havre and seems disconnected from the rest of the film. If her scenes had been excised completely, it wouldn't have had an adverse effect on the film. However, all the other main protagonists are involved in the big final action in the Tunisian desert. And most of them don't make it, falling victim to bombs, bullets, landmines, exploding shells, etc.

The Biggest Battle is cluttered and often lacks focus. Characters are introduced only to disappear for long stretches. It's hard to work out who the main character is supposed to be, or indeed if there even *is* a main character at all. Lovelock or Gemma would seem to be the nominal heroes, but Keach and Berger also demonstrate heroic and sympathetic qualities on the German side.

In fact, one of the things I liked about the movie is that it doesn't paint a picture of 100% good Allies and 100% evil Nazis. There are some shades of grey with almost every character - little flaws or traits which prevent us from totally liking or loathing them, making them that bit more believable.

There are too many story strands, but everything does eventually tie together as the movie enters its closing stages. Perhaps the most compelling vignette is the Keach/Eggar segment. It helps that they seem to be genuinely trying to do something with the hackneyed material. Keach called the film "flat-out awful" in his autobiography, but his performance conveys a fair sense of moral turmoil, self-doubt and tormented allegiance. Likewise, Eggar has a certain stubborn pride and sense of honour which is tragically admirable. Gemma's action heroics provide some gung-ho enjoyment too, though in the English version his dubbed voice (slightly uppercrust Queen's English, tonally bland) is unintentionally funny. Fonda is pretty good too, though the role makes no specific demands of him. Fenech, on the other hand, is really wasted, and Berger merely glowers intensely in most of his scenes. Lovelock is called upon to pout and look boyishly handsome, and he's rather outclassed by the big guns. Huston shows open contempt for the film, almost marching off the set in a big tantrum in his final scene. It might just be the way it's edited, but one gets the sense he's giving the crew and other cast members the middle finger as he exits the picture. "To think they said I was too old for all this," he sneers derisively. "Truth is, all you chaps are too young. Well, see you around!" He then ambles calmly into a hail of enemy shelling and is promptly blown to smithereens.

Lenzi would go on to make another surprisingly starry war epic the following year, *From Hell to Victory* with George Peppard, George Hamilton, Capucine, Horst Buccholz, Sam Wanamaker and Jean-Pierre Cassel. His massively offensive, controversial and profitable cannibal opus *Cannibal Ferox* (1981) was just round the corner too and would forever cement his infamy.

The Biggest Battle has some decent action punctuated with stock footage, a few interesting performances and character vignettes, and a catchy military march score by Lenzi's frequent composer of choice Franco Micalizzi. On the flip side, it is quite muddled and tries to cover way more than is possible in the modest running time. I'd be lying if I said it was good, but it has its moments if you're willing to give it a chance.

And *that* cast... on a curiosity level alone, '70s movie nuts will salivate at the chance to see so many top players under one roof. File *The Biggest Battle* under 'Loads-Of-Big-Stars-In-A-Pic-Nobody-Has-Ever-Heard-Of', and save it for a day when you've nothing better to do.

Cut-Throats Nine

by Darren Linder

"What good is that, Sergeant? No one's getting out of this alive."

Spaghetti westerns went through quite a transformation in the '70s. Trying to make a quick profit, entries of decreasing quality were churned out by the dozen which resulted in a glut on the market. The genre was in its death throes, and filmmakers were forced to invent new variations like the comedic western (e.g. the *Trinity* films), the Zapata western (set during the Mexican Revolution), gothic Euro westerns, and overtly political westerns. *Cut-Throats Nine*, a violent and bloody Spanish offering, was made in 1972 and marks two unusual genres being combined in an attempt to stay relevant and interesting. It's a perfect example of what you might call a 'horror-western'. It also exemplifies another small subgenre known as the 'Chorizo Western' (which basically means a western filmed in Spain by a Spanish director, instead of a production that has the usual Italian links).

Joaquín Luis Romero Marchent gives us a unique vision with *Cut-Throats Nine*. It combines two of my favorite genres, though I suspect it will not appeal to everyone. If you are mainly a fan of traditional fare like *High Noon, Shane* and *The Searchers,* you should perhaps steer clear of this one! *Cut-Throats Nine* is best described as a combination of a Sergio Leone spaghetti western and a Lucio Fulci horror film - ghoulish, gory and batshit crazy! It will appeal to anyone who likes films which teeter on the edge, like *Four of the Apocalypse* and *Django Kill... If You Live, Shoot!* Many movies stick to the established norms of what should happen according to the conventions of the genre, but it's refreshing to come across something like *Cut-Throats Nine* where expectations are thrown out the window. In fact, all three spaghetti entries mentioned above drew me in with their weirdness, and I was unable to predict what would happen next. Combining the western and horror genres is a genius move which, sadly, hasn't been done often enough. The only recent examples I absolutely loved were *Dead Birds* (2004) and *Bone Tomahawk* (2015).

The plot is pretty simple but has numerous layers which are uncovered as it progresses. A group of prisoners are being transported to jail, supervised by some soldiers travelling in a stagecoach. The prisoners are chained together and there seems to be more to them than first suspected. Several have shared history, or know each other, and this is revealed via interesting flashbacks. Bandits attack the group and kill some of the soldiers. They search the coach for the gold they thought was inside but find nothing. The bandits run the coach off the road, destroying it. The remaining seven prisoners, plus the Sergeant and his daughter, head out on foot in the snow with the horses.

An intriguing development occurs about thirty minutes in when everyone learns the gold the bandits couldn't find is actually still there. The thick chains and leg-irons which keep the prisoners attached to each other are actually made of gold. It has been painted over to avoid detection! Now the prisoners need to find a way to overtake their captor and get away with their own chains of gold. The very shackles they've been trying to get out of are now what they want to take with them for financial gain. The Sergeant, still trying to contain and control the convicts, could just kill them all and take the gold. The prisoners know this, but it turns out the Sergeant won't bump them off yet as he is trying to determine the identity of one of them so he can avenge a past wrong.

The cast doesn't feature anyone you're likely to have seen before, which is rather refreshing as there are no preconceived expectations of who will live or die. All the prisoners are played by believable actors, and their motivations and allegiances change as certain histories are revealed. The main character, played by Robert Hundar, has a grizzled, desperate Charlton Heston vibe. Inexplicably and unwisely, he's brought his daughter along and is tasked with keeping her out of peril. It's like a 'Take Your Daughter to Work Day' gone horribly wrong. She is played by Emma Cohen, who does a great job in a tough role. Her big, innocent eyes and youthful, porcelain face provide a perfect contrast to the whiskered faces and dirty, weathered skin of the men. There is a powerful shot of her expression as she looks at her father just after he kills a man. Her gaze conveys the respect she has lost for him, the shattered fairytale of her father being the perfect protector, innocence lost.

As the group tries to survive the wintry weather without shelter or supplies, they trudge along like characters from some twisted Jack London story. The film shares a certain something with other snow-bound entries like *The Great Silence, McCabe and Mrs. Miller* and *Jeremiah Johnson*. The characters have to sparingly use what few bullets they possess to hunt deer in order to eat. There is an impressive scene of four horses falling in the snow while attached to the coach. This made me raise my eyebrows - I wondered if the stunt had been performed in a safe way that protected the animals. Inevitably a horse falls and breaks its leg while traversing the mountains and they have to mercy kill it. Then a member of the chain gang dies, and somebody hacks off his foot with a machete so they can continue without the dead weight. I love how this film feels very claustrophobic, even though much of it occurs outside. The claustrophobia comes from them being cut off from the outside world, forced to rely on each other for survival. It feels like a stage play with nine main characters who are in every scene together (until they start dying). Like many spaghettis, it offers little hope or redemption. There are many images of sweaty, bearded faces squinting into the light. As more characters die, it comes to resemble a *Ten Little Indians* scenario, as we wonder who, if anyone, will survive the nightmarish ordeal.

If you've seen Quentin Tarantino's 2015 film *The Hateful Eight*, you will recognize where he got much of his inspiration. The grizzled lawman escorting a prisoner in chains on a stagecoach in snowy weather... the characters they bring aboard that have hidden motives for being there... the second half of the film taking place primarily in wood cabins with people hiding their history from each other... the graphic and visceral violence and the lack of any truly 'good' character to root for... the exploitation feel... revenge upon revenge upon revenge. I guarantee Tarantino watched *Cut-Throats Nine* and loved it, using it as strong inspiration for *The Hateful Eight*.

It's worth mentioning the infamous violence. There is a good deal of it, and it is indeed graphic. If you've seen any of Lucio Fulci's horror films, you'll know what to expect. Fulci earned the nickname 'The Godfather of Gore' thanks to his output in the '70s and '80s (*Zombie, The Beyond, The House by the Cemetery, City of the Living Dead, The New York Ripper*, etc.) Narrative flow and character logic weren't a big concern for him, but showy, gory kills were a different matter. They were the centerpieces around which his movies were built. He reveled in showing the method of death in close-up detail, not cutting away like most directors would. He didn't believe your mind would fill the gaps and make scenes more violent than they actually were. He wanted to show the gore in all its glory,

and it was up to you to look away if you couldn't handle it. The death scenes in *Cut-Throats Nine* feel like that. There are deaths by stabbing, shooting, burning, throat-slashing, choking, bludgeoning and other methods.

One particular death scene had me rewinding the disc to rewatch it a few times. A character is shot point-blank in the face, and the makeup crew deliver a truly shocking special effect. His eye appears to be slightly dislodged from its socket and the wound pulses out blood like it would from arterial pressure. It's like something out of a horror film, and I was hugely impressed how realistic they made it look. Today they would use phony-looking CGI to add fake blood, or possibly even just digitally animate the entire facial wound. But in 1972, they did it old-school, using an exquisite makeup job, prosthetics and hidden pneumatic tubes to pulse fake blood. It's an astonishing death scene, one of many contained within the movie.

My favorite scene occurs about an hour in. One of the chain-gang convicts escapes into a snowstorm carrying his gold chains and some provisions which he has stolen from the group. He starts hallucinating, either from being drunk or dehydrated and feverish. The director gives us four quick flashes of animals that the character reacts to seeing in his bewildered condition. They are an owl, a vulture, a raven and a Komodo dragon. I learned from a quick bit of research that these animals were not selected at random just to freak the character out. They are, in fact, quite symbolic and mean something to this character and the story overall.

1) The Owl can be a warning of evil and death. Some Native American tribes believe it is a psychopomp, a creature that sends the living to the afterlife.

2) Vultures feed on carrion, and are often seen circling above a creature that is about to die. They are considered a bad omen.

3) Ravens are also carrion eaters and can represent death. They are considered psychopomps and tricksters.

4) The Komodo dragon is an apex predator which dominates the ecosystems in which it lives. It symbolizes survival instincts and warrior energy.

This character has been involved with a group of men fighting over who is the alpha male. He goes on to try to use his own warrior strength to escape his situation, although he is haunted by death all around him. His face looks feral and desperate like a cornered animal. He has broken the code of his seedy brotherhood, and there is absolutely no honor among these thieves.

After he hallucinates the four totem animals, he comes across the ruins of a burned house. Although the smoke seems to be moving back down into the rubble, he continues watching and we recognize that this is indeed backwards footage of a burning house collapsing. Since it goes backwards, the structure appears to rebuild itself like in a dream. Seeing a burning building reconstruct itself in the snow is a mesmerizing and surreal scene that makes the movie for me. There is no music to accompany this bizarre visual, just the sound of the wind, then the breathing of the panicking character. Its oddness made me think of the visual poetry of the movies of Russian director Andrei Tarkovsky. Tarkovsky helmed two films where characters watch entire buildings burn down: *Mirror* (1975) and *The Sacrifice* (1986). And much like the fire-in-the-snow imagery, Tarkovsky wanted his scenes of burning buildings to involve water. In *Mirror*, water drips steadily off the roof of the house as the other building burns. The woman goes to the well and drinks water and splashes her face with it as the building is engulfed. In *The Sacrifice*, the building burns on the shore of a lake, and the surrounding yard is filled with huge puddles which people splash through as they watch the house ablaze. Opposing elements. Fire and water. Present and past. I sincerely doubt Tarkovsky ever watched *Cut-Throats Nine*, but it is an interesting connection.

And just to take this scene into even more insane territory, once the building rebuilds itself, we recognize it as the cabin where they left another character to die in a fire. That very character then appears out of the smoke, impossibly standing in front with burn wounds on him. He is like a wraith from an Edgar Allan Poe story, wanting revenge, shambling towards the terrified convict. In a flash, the film just turned into a horror movie with a stalking zombie-ghost back from the dead. Did the burned character somehow survive the fire? Or is the convict hallucinating this too, ridden with guilt for killing him? I won't explain any further, but this eerie sequence is, I believe, the highlight of the movie, a stunning scene which demonstrates bravura filmmaking. It fits into the narrative structure perfectly. It's more than just a trippy midnight movie gimmick that has been thoughtlessly throw in.

Much of the story is told in flashbacks, involving going back in time. All memories are transporting you backwards. So many characters commit atrocities from which they cannot return. The theme of going back in time to relive happy moments, or to undo some heinous act of violence, streams through the entire movie. So, showing this footage of the building burning in reverse, recreating and rebuilding itself, makes complete sense. You cannot unburn a house that you burned down, nor can you bring a person you've killed back to life. The character realizes he is out alone in the elements with no supplies or weapons to survive. He starts seeing totem animals that are all bad omens, and sees the man he thought was murdered coming after him. He certainly wishes he could go back and undo the things that led him here. The desire for a reversal, a yearning for second chances, is shared by most of the characters. It's a fascinating and haunting scene with more depth and meaning than it might seem upon first viewing.

There is one little touch that I appreciated on my second or third viewing. Some of the characters start singing the song *Oh My Darling, Clementine*, which was famously used in the 1946 John Ford western of the same name starring Henry Fonda. Euro westerns were often critical of American oaters, often deconstructing the American western template. They were nihilistic and sought to demythologize the American approach to the genre, showing instead their darker, greedier, genocidal, more sociopathic nature. They felt like a direct response to the works of Howard Hawks and John Ford which typically starred John Wayne. By including such a classic song and having the main characters alter the lyrics to make it crass and nonsensical, Marchent is clearly thumbing his nose at the older traditional westerns. Like the characters bastardizing the western song, this film - and, indeed, most spaghetti westerns - revel in bastardizing the predictable mores and tropes of traditional westerns.

Cut-Throats Nine has a great gloomy soundtrack, immersive cinematography and strikingly beautiful locations. I can't recommend it enough, especially for cult western fans. I loved the themes of father figures, shifting power dynamics, competition for the alpha male role, holding grudges, innocence and bloody revenge. It's a sadistic film which still packs a big punch and is unlike anything you've ever seen. Sign up for an unforgettable journey through hell across the snow. Load your bullets, grab your machete... and trust no one!

There have been plans to film a remake of this movie for over a decade now. The actors attached to the project currently are Harvey Keitel, Mads Mikkelsen, and Jordi Mollà with Rodrigo Gudiño directing. Much as I dislike unnecessary remakes, I am pretty intrigued by this one. Maybe watch the original first though, so you know what you're getting into!

Bless The Beasts & Children

Summer Camp Blues Coming of Age with Bless the Beasts and Children

by John Harrison

For me, Stanley Kramer's *Bless the Beasts and Children* (1971) has long stood as one of the great unsung American films of its decade. I first encountered it on late night television back in the '70s. It would have been during the school holidays no doubt, when I was allowed to set up a camp bed in the lounge and watch all-night movie marathons to my heart's content. These were the lengths a young film fanatic would go to in those pre-home video years to make sure he caught a movie that may not get repeated for years. Even when I managed to stay awake until the film came on, I would have to endure local telesales evangelists like ssi Dye cutting in halfway through with some 20-minute advertorial selling an orange vinyl couch or flared polyester men's suit. I just remember sitting there screaming at the TV to get on with it.

So, *Bless the Beasts and Children* was one of those films I'd never heard of when it showed up at some ungodly hour. It instantly transfixed me in much the same way as Cornel Wilde's strange African survival film *The Naked Prey* (1965), which I also caught late at night when I was very young. Looking back, I can see a number of reasons why *Bless the Beasts and Children* resonated so strongly with me. The basic premise was instantly involving: at an Arizona summer boy's camp, six of the so-called losers - dubbed the Bedwetters - decide to prove their worth, to themselves as much as anybody else, by breaking out of camp one evening and embarking on a trek to set free a herd of buffalo who are scheduled to be slaughtered by a group of hunters the following day. In their ensuing journey to the killing fields, the six boys - all from financially well-off but emotionally crippled homes - learn more about life and friendship than any parent or camp counsellor could ever hope to teach. They are also, of course, forced to face the harsh realities and ramifications of their well-meaning but spur-of-the-moment actions.

Being around the same age as the six lead characters no doubt played a huge part in the impact it had on me when I first saw it. I was never treated in school the same way the poor Bedwetters were, but I could certainly empathise with them and their feelings of self-doubt. It was also around this time that I took my first family vacation to the United States where I visited and fell in love with the starkly beautiful, otherworldly Arizona landscape which features so prominently in the film. I was absorbing a lot of offbeat American culture at the time and developing a fascination towards its mobile home landscapes and small-town strangeness (something which I think was nurtured on that first American vacation). I can still vividly recall our tour bus stopping in a rather small dry Arizona town for lunch, and seeing the local patrol car driving around with a bumper sticker which read "Support Your Local Hooker."

All this goes a long way in explaining

why *Bless the Beasts and Children* struck such a lasting chord with me. But there was also a strange quality to it which made it more than just another coming-of-age story. It reflects, at times, a vibe of undefinable weirdness comparable to William Golding's 'Lord of the Flies' and its 1963 film adaptation. This oddness is conveyed not just thematically but by some stark and disturbing visual cues, such as the stuffed heads of native American animals given out to the various cabins as some sick totem of achievement, and the inclusion of genuine buffalo slaughter footage, which is fleeting but does appear at several points. This footage is hard to take, but isn't exploitative and is quite important in establishing the stark brutality behind the lead characters' motivations. There's also a rather peculiar, voyeuristic, homoerotic undertone with the young campers often parading through the woods in nothing but their Y-fronts (along with a shot of several of the Bedwetters masturbating in their bunks at the same time, a moment used for comic effect).

Bless the Beasts and Children is based on a 1970 novel by Michigan-born Glendon Swarthout (1918-1992). He dabbled in a wide range of genres, other filmic adaptations including *Where the Boys Are* (1960), one of the first movies to document the romanticised adventures of college girls on spring break (a modernised remake was filmed in 1984) and the classic Duke western *The Shootist* (1976), which was directed by Don Siegel. *Bless the Beasts and Children* was Swarthout's most successful novel, certainly in terms of sales, and has rarely - if ever - been out of print in the United States. It was regularly found on school reading lists (I first read it a year or so after seeing the movie, when it was assigned to us in class). The story was inspired by the adventures of Swarthout's son when he was a high school student and summer camp counsellor. When the book was first published, it generated something of a bidding war over film rights. Stanley Kramer eventually won and quickly set about cutting a deal with Columbia Pictures to produce and direct it.

Kramer by this point was a veteran Hollywood heavyweight with such classics as *The Defiant Ones* (1958), *On the Beach* (1959), *Inherit the Wind* (1960), *Judgement at Nuremberg* (1961), *It's a Mad, Mad, Mad, Mad World* (1963) and *Guess Who's Coming to Dinner* (1967) under his belt. He seems a strange choice to bring *Bless the Beasts and Children* to the screen - the story at first glance seems better suited to one of the up-and-coming young turks of early '70s American cinema. But he did have a reputation for delivering big 'message' movies, and it was clear from his previous film *R.P.M.* (1970) - a drama set against the backdrop of radical student activism - that he was interested in exploring themes that were relevant and important to younger audiences. Following *Bless the Beasts and Children*, he would only direct three further features, including the uneven thriller *The Domino Principal* (1977) and an adaptation of the Broadway play *The Runner Stumbles* (1979).

Charged with adapting Swarthout's novel for the screen was Mac Benoff, whose resumé consisted mostly of writing episodes of '50s TV shows like *The Eddie Fisher Show* and *Make Room for Daddy*. He also co-wrote the final Marx Brothers film, *Love Happy* (1949), which illustrates just how far back his career stretched. *Bless the Beasts and Children* would turn out to be his final screenplay credit, and he died the year after it was released. Benoff's script stays pretty close to Swarthout's novel, using the same structure and style, with frequent flashbacks to establish character and explain motivations and backgrounds. The flashbacks also help to break things up neatly, adding touches of humour at the right moments and creating a nice beat to the story. Because the book was rather slim at under 200 pages, it could be adapted without having the usual problem of deciding what to drop due to running time constraints. Benoff manages to tell the book's story very effectively within the film's 109 minutes, penning a fairly literal and faithful adaptation. However, one notable sequence from the novel doesn't make it into the film - the scene where the Bedwetters defy camp orders, steal some horses and ride into town to watch a western at the local drive-in. They see the Burt Lancaster/Lee Marvin classic *The Professionals* (1966), which serves as a dry run for their big adventure and goes a long way toward explaining where they got the courage to undertake their mission to save the buffalo.

The film also extends the timeframe of the events. In Swarthout's novel, the main story unfolds over a single night and morning. The same events on screen take place over a couple of nights and days, which probably made sense from a filmmaking perspective, since it saves having whole chunks of the action taking place in darkness. As it is, one of the technical drawbacks is that several of the night scenes were obviously filmed 'day-for-night' with cinematographer Michel Hugo using tinted lenses to make it appear darker. The shadows caused by the blazing Arizona sun are clearly evident in certain shots when it is supposedly the dead of night. Despite this, Hugo manages to capture a strong visual flavour, both in the intimate moments as well as the grand scenic scenes, where he paints some stunning panoramic vistas.

No doubt one of the strongest elements of this adaptation and the reason it creates such an emotional punch is the amazing cast of young actors assembled to bring the six central characters to life. These are headed by Barry Robins as John Cotton, the self-appointed leader of the group who dreams of following in the footsteps of his military father and lives with his divorced mother, a forty-something social animal who is terrified of aging. In many ways, she resents her son because he represents a symbol of her advancing age. As Swarthout writes in his novel: "To remain a girl, she had to keep her son a boy."

SPOILER WARNING: One significant change the film makes from Swarthout's book is in the way Cotton meets his tragic demise. On screen, he is accidently killed by a shot from one of the hunters trying to stop him from stampeding the buffalo herd by driving a hotwired pick-up truck towards them. In the novel, he is killed when he drives the truck over a ridge and crashes it into a deep ravine.

Robins was born in Brooklyn and attended New York's High School of Performing Arts, as well as studying under the famous acting teacher Stella Adler. His first real taste of success came in the 1963 Chicago production of *The King and I*, where his performance as the Crown Prince so impressed composer Richard Rodgers - of Rodgers and Hammerstein fame - that he personally invited Robins to reprise the role at the play's New York revival the following year. Apart from a very prolific career in theatre, he also appeared in episodic television shows like *Twelve O'Clock High*, *The Girl from U.N.C.L.E.*, *Rat Patrol* and *Columbo*, and was one of the many young actors to audition for *The Monkees* in 1966. Robins also spent time as a cocktail lounge entertainer and wrote an unproduced screenplay in 1977 called *Our Days at M.A.D.*, looking back at his experiences at the High School of Performing Arts.

But it's *Bless the Beasts and Children* that remains the actor's tour de force. He was already 26 by the time he played the role of Cotton, a full ten years older than the character, yet he is totally convincing in the role. He comes across passionate, caring and tough, with a fierce determination that crosses into obsession, even possession. What a tragedy that he died of complications from HIV in 1986 at the terribly young age of 41, but what an amazing role he left behind for people to remember him for. Interestingly, Robins' nephew claims his uncle's unproduced *Our Days at M.A.D.* screenplay was stolen by

writer Chris Gore, who turned it into the hit movie *Fame* (1980), but Robins was already getting sick at this point and was too weak to pursue any legal action.

The most recognisable and experienced member of the young cast is Bill Mumy, who plays habitual auto thief Lawrence Teft. Mumy was only 17 but already a veteran of American television, thanks mostly to his role as Will Robinson in Irwin Allen's classic sci-fi series *Lost in Space*, which ran between 1965 and 1968 and remained very popular in re-runs. It was something of a surprise to see him go from a squeaky-clean kid to a gangly, pimply teen with long stringy red hair who spouts dialogue like: "Shove it up your anal orifice!" Apart from *Lost in Space*, Mumy also appeared in some great instalments of *Alfred Hitchcock Presents* and *The Twilight Zone*, including the classic *It's a Good Life* episode in which a child terrorizes a small town with his psychic powers. (Mumy also had a role in the Joe Dante-directed remake of this story for the *Twilight Zone* movie in 1982, a story which was homaged in a great 1991 Halloween episode of *The Simpsons*). At the time of filming, Mumy was branching out into music and fronted his own country-blues band called Redwood. One of Redwood's songs called *Beautiful Day* (written by Mumy) finds its way into *Bless the Beasts and Children*, when the kids vocalize it while driving through the Arizona desert en route to their destination.

Miles Chapin plays Sammy Schecker, the overweight comedian of the group. He uses humour as a protective shield for himself as a means of relieving tension whenever the Bedwetters are starting to doubt themselves, making his character very central and important to the story. In the film, Schecker is the son of a famous Jewish Las Vegas comedian, which helps explain where all his bad jokes come from. After *Bless the Beasts and Children*, Chapin slimmed down and appeared in movies like *Hair* (1979), Tobe Hooper's *The Funhouse* (1981) and the George Lucas/Marvel Comics misfire *Howard the Duck* (1986). He also did some work for director Milos Forman in the late '90s, appearing in the biopics *The People .vs. Larry Flynt* (1996) and *Man on the Moon* (1999).

Playing the Lally brothers are Bob Kramer and Marc Vahanian. Kramer was no relation to director Stanley, and had a brief acting career that mostly entailed appearances on TV shows like *The Partridge Family* and *Nanny and the Professor*. He also appeared as Johnny in the classic 1971 *Brady Bunch* episode *Where There's Smoke*, playing one of the members of a high school rock band that pressures squeaky clean Greg Brady (Barry Williams) into smoking a cigarette. Vanahian's career was somewhat more extensive and included a lot of TV work as well as appearances in *The Amityville Horror* (1979) and the violent revenge actioner *Exterminator 2* (1984).

The last of the six young cast members is Darel Glaser as Gerald Goodenow, the frail blonde moppet who comes across somewhat effeminately. As fragile as a sparrow, he is the only actual bedwetter amongst the group. There's a touching and wonderfully played out flashback scene showing how Cotton is the only kid in camp who extends a helping hand to Goodenow and welcomes him into the Bedwetters' cabin, where he will be safe. Glaser's on-screen career was rather limited after his debut in *Bless the Beasts and Children*. Apart from one-off appearances on *Marcus Welby, M.D.* and *Shazam!*, his only other film credits are bit-parts in the Steve McQueen flick *An Enemy of the People* (1978) and a telemovie called *The Cheerleaders* (1976), which was directed by Richard Crenna.

Apart from the six young central performances, there are a number of supporting roles that are well-cast and important to the plot. There's Jesse White as Shecker's father, the loud and obnoxious polyester lounge comedian, concerned more with how his son reflects on himself than how the poor kid actually feels; Ken Swofford as Wheaties, the Bedwetters' camp cabin master who has given up in disgust on his charges and treats them just as cruelly as the other kids at the camp (he is also one of the eager buffalo hunters whom the Bedwetters despise so much); and Elaine Devry as Cotton's mother, the single mom terrified of aging and losing her looks - she is wonderfully effective in her one scene (though she does also appear briefly in the pre-credits dream sequence).

The standout among all the adult actors is easily Bruce Glover, real-life father of Crispin, who proves that oddness runs in the family. In *Bless the Beasts and Children*, he has a small but very memorable role as one of two redneck hustlers who torment the Bedwetters when they pull into a greasy diner for burgers and shakes. While Wayne Sutherlin as the other redneck plays his role with more obvious aggression, Glover comes across as the one to be most wary of. There is a great tipsy playfulness about his character that is both humorous and unnerving, with the threat of violence bubbling under the surface. Glover has stated in interviews that he believes this performance landed him his best-known role as one of the homosexual hitmen in *Diamonds are Forever* (1971) later that same year. Glover had started his career in varied fare like the kooky *Frankenstein Meets the Space Monster* (1965), *The Thomas Crown Affair* (1968), *Dayton's Devils* (1968) and *C.C. and Company* (1970). Post-*Bless the Beasts and Children*, he appeared in *Walking Tall* (1973), *Chinatown* (1974), *Hard Times* (1975), *Night of the Scarecrow* (1995) and *Ghost World* (2001).

The soundtrack, composed by Barry De Vorzon and Perry Botkin, Jnr., provides an integral part of the emotional core, and is highlighted by the title theme, which was written by De Vorzon and Botkin, Jnr., and performed by the popular brother/sister pop duo The Carpenters. The piano-based ballad, which is heard throughout in both vocal and instrumental versions, proved a minor hit for The Carpenters, reaching Number 67 on the US Billboard charts. It was nominated for an Academy Award in the 'Best Song' category in 1972 but lost out to Issac Hayes' funky *Theme from Shaft* (if you are going to lose out to any film theme, I guess *that* is the one to lose to). It really is a lovely composition, given a heartfelt vocal by Karen Carpenter which, like a lot of The Carpenters' music, carries extra emotional weight in light of the singer's tragic early death at the age of 32 (the first high-profile death to be attributed to anorexia nervosa).

There is also *Cotton's Dream*, a beautiful instrumental piece used at several crucial points throughout. When listened to within the context of the movie, it is incredibly moving. When listened to purely as a piece of music, it still remains dramatic and inspirational. In fact, when ABC's *Wide World of Sports* played it over a montage of the famous Romanian gymnast Nadia Comăneci performing her routines at the 1976 Summer Olympics, it proved so popular that it was re-titled *Nadia's Theme* and issued as single, hitting the American Top 10 that year. It has also become famous as the opening theme music to the long-running daytime soap *The Young and the Restless*. They also used the Carpenters' theme song from *Bless the Beasts and Children* on a 1982 episode of *The Young and the Restless*, in a scene where David Hasselhoff's character had to say goodbye to his son as he left to live with his stepdad. But the music was originally conceived and composed for *Bless the Beasts and Children*, and that is how it deserves to be remembered and appreciated. De Vorzon was a very prolific soundtrack composer who worked as the music supervisor for blaxploitation flicks like *Slaughter's Big Rip-Off* (1973) and *Hell Up in Harlem* (1973). He provided the music for a diverse list of movies that include *Rolling Thunder* (1977), *The Warriors* (1979), *Xanadu* (1980) *Mr. Mom* (1983), *Night of the Creeps* (1986) and *Exorcist III* (1990). De Vorzon also lends his vocal talent to the *Bless the Beasts and Children* soundtrack, singing *Down the Line*, a soft pop/rock track that is played as the Bedwetters experience the excitement of exploring a townscape free from adult supervision.

In 1972, a truncated 14-minute version of *Bless the Beasts and Children*, renamed *Love to Kill*, was part of a 1972 educational/guidance series titled *Searching for Values*, produced by the Learning Corporation of America. 16mm prints of this series were sent around American high schools to be screened in class, no doubt under the guise of them having some educational benefit. You can imagine it being shown as part of a social guidance class, or as a time-filler to keep students occupied when a teacher called in sick. With a title like *Love to Kill*, it's hard to tell exactly what sort of lesson they were trying to teach with this truncated film. It pretty much condensed the heart of the story and its main beats, without using any of the exposition or flashback sequences.

The original theatrical trailer was quite interesting and somewhat different and daring. Rather than follow a traditional trailer format, it is structured like a mock live television debate about the issue of gun control, ownership and responsibility, with Bill Mumy (credited as himself) facing off against a fellow named Floyd Crebbs, who supposedly represents the American Gun Cult Association, but is clearly meant to be symbolic of the National Rifle Association, or NRA. "We condemn the movie *Bless the Beasts and Children* because it is a vicious attack upon the hunters of America," Crebbs argues, his confident demeanour slowly turning into a sweaty, nervous ness as the trailer progresses. He starts to crumble in the face of Mumy's innocently childlike, brutally honest opinion of hunters who kill purely for sport. It's a strange, somewhat experimental trailer, which bravely tries to sell the movie to a wide audience. However, America's huge number of gun advocates may have been put off since the trailer pretty much spells out how fiercely anti-gun the film's themes and messages are going to be.

It's a pity that *Love to Kill* and the trailer for *Bless the Beasts and Children* were not included on the official Sony DVD release in 2012. They were, however, both included on the DVD-R release that was put out by Shocking Videos in the early 2000s, and the trailer can be found on YouTube. The film is desperately in need of a Blu-ray release but it's rumoured rights issues over the use of *Cotton's Theme* has prevented it from being issued in that format thus far. Which is a shame, as it's a piece of music that was written specifically for the movie, so it would be outrageous if any label or studio tried to replace it for any home video release.

Unfortunately, despite the popularity of the novel, the film version of *Bless the Beasts and Children* did not prove a box-office success after having its world premiere at the 1971 Berlin Film Festival. Russian critics viewed it as scathing indictment of the massacres at Kent State University and My Lai in Vietnam, though the film is more an overall criticism against America's cult of gun worship which, as previously mentioned, may have been one of the reasons it didn't do very well upon release. It was also an extremely hard film to define, with its mixture of pre-*Meatballs* summer camp comedy, *Lord of the Flies*-style strangeness, and social commentary. But it is a movie which, if it clicks and connects with you, can be a highly rewarding and powerfully moving viewing experience.

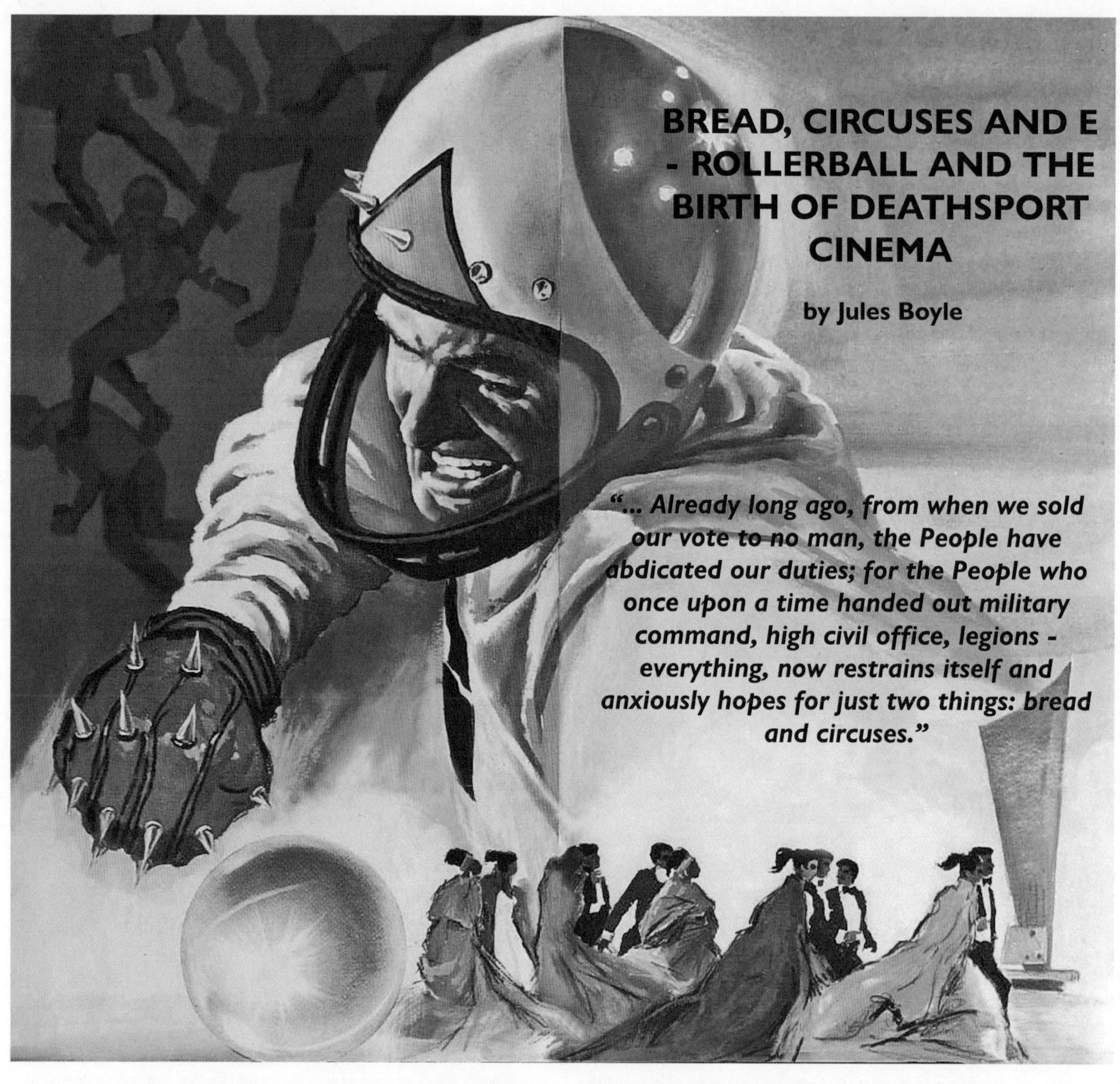

BREAD, CIRCUSES AND E - ROLLERBALL AND THE BIRTH OF DEATHSPORT CINEMA

by Jules Boyle

"... Already long ago, from when we sold our vote to no man, the People have abdicated our duties; for the People who once upon a time handed out military command, high civil office, legions - everything, now restrains itself and anxiously hopes for just two things: bread and circuses."

It seems as long as there has been sport of any kind, there has been an idea that it can be used to distract the masses. We can go back over 2000 years, to the time of the Roman poet Juvenal for the famous quote above, and probably keep on going back. There's evidence of Paleolithic tribes wrestling and swimming as a competitive sport painted on a wall in a cave in France 15,300 years ago. What's the betting at least some of those games were organised by the tribal elders to deflect from the fact they had lost the secret of fire or were hogging all the mammoth meat?

Anyone who's into watching sport will tell you that, at its best, it can be a transcendent experience. It unites people with a common goal, and they experience the same ecstatic highs and devastating lows, sometimes minutes apart. It's something that brings humans together, from all walks of life, for a cause which matters to them all equally. Believe it or not, it can be a beautiful thing.

Of course, there's a flipside to this. The very nature of competitive sport is tribal at its heart. If you support a team in one half of the city, you naturally hate the team in the other half. Since the day it was invented, a subsection of football fans have enjoyed battering each other as much as they enjoy watching the game itself. Rivalry and passion at sport thrive on conflict; it's only human. Then there's the general bloodlust that comes with watching the games, whatever they are. Never mind the bloodlust from cheering a meaty tackle in a game of football or rugby. From ancient Roman gladiators to modern-day MMA fighters, we love seeing our fellow man properly hurting each other.

So, it stands to reason that a long time before a wise

man identified television as "the drug of the nation", the masses were regularly being swept along by some sporting event when their attention might have been better spent somewhere else.

Fast forward to the early '70s. Faith in elected leaders and governments was at a low ebb. The war in Vietnam had brought the sinister and undemocratic nature of the military-industrial complex into the spotlight. Richard Nixon's public downfall after the Watergate scandal proved that you couldn't trust anyone, not even the POTUS. The counterculture had long seen The Man as the enemy, but the seeds of mistrust had grown over the years to the extent that the idea of politicians, corporations, the super-rich and the authorities in general not having our best interests at heart was less outlandish with every new incident.

In 1973 William Harrison, a professor of Creative Writing at the University of Arkansas, witnessed a particularly violent brawl at a university basketball game. Already deeply concerned with the shifting social and economic situations in America at the time, he was inspired by the incident to bring all these ideas together for a short story called 'Roller Ball Murder'. In its brief page count, it showed a world controlled by a handful of corporations, with a compliant population dulled into obedience by means of a hyper-violent spectator sport - the eponymous Roller Ball. Told from the perspective of Jonathan E, the greatest player the game has ever seen, it's a bleak but engaging vision of a dystopian future. Despite its big ideas, it isn't all that far-fetched.

The two-time Academy Award-nominated director Norman Jewison certainly didn't think so. The man behind huge hits like *In the Heat of the Night* (1967), *Fiddler on the Roof* (1971) and *Jesus Christ Superstar* (1973) had relocated from his native Canada to London and became a regular at Chelsea FC's home ground Stamford Bridge, where he observed first-hand the dawn of what would become proper football violence from their supporters and the visiting away fans. By sheer coincidence, Harrison was also resident in London at the time, so Jewison got in touch with an offer to buy the rights to his story. An initial offer of $50,000 was rebuffed, with the unknown author countering with a higher sum and the caveat that he be allowed to write the script. Surprisingly to Harrison, his terms were deemed acceptable and pre-production commenced before anyone had even told him it was a goer.

Jewison and Harrison would go on to spend months together in London, working out how to expand his short story for the big screen, plus the rules of the game they would be building it around. This was no half-baked fake sport that would be led by the narrative. Rollerball (now one word for maximum punchiness) was fully realised, to the extent that they would receive offers to bring it into the real world after the film's release.

Working with a modest budget of £5-6 million, Jewison spent a large percentage of it building a single Rollerball track in Munich's Olympiastadion, a futuristic (for the time) stadium that had been constructed for the 1972

Olympic Games. The cast would mostly consist of unknowns, such as Maud Adams in the female lead role and John Houseman, better known for his work writing the screenplay for *Citizen Kane (*1941). Ralph Richardson had a huge pedigree, but his role was merely a small if pivotal one as an unnamed librarian. The star quality that helped get *Rollerball* noticed would come from one man - James Caan.

The New Yorker was a household name after scene-stealing turns in *Brian's Song* (1970), *The Godfather* (1971) and *The Gambler* (1974), all of which saw him nominated for (if not actually winning) Emmys, Academy Awards and Golden Globes. *Rollerball* might not have been a big movie, but the presence of James Caan made it one. Relocating to California, the actor and his new teammates (and their opposing numbers), as well as the stuntmen who would bolster their ranks, spent four full months learning to play Rollerball. It was something they would become fully committed to, to the extent that when the cameras finally rolled in Munich, they were playing the game for real and with Jewison's blessing. Naturally, injuries were commonplace, including Caan himself who insisted on doing his own stunts, even after he had cracked a rib and dislocated his shoulder. A full-on, no-holds-barred game was allowed after filming was completed, but much like the movie's grand finale, it was carnage... and scoring goals came a distant second to knocking the hell out of each other.

Rollerball would be released in July, 1975, but a few months before, another film directly inspired by it would actually beat Jewison's film to the dystopian futuresport punch. Legendary low-budget filmmaker Roger Corman rarely missed an opportunity to crank out a cash-in, and when he caught wind of the upcoming 'society-kept-placid-by-deathsports' film he rushed his own into production to take full advantage.

Based on screenwriter Ib Melchior's 1956 short story 'The Racer', *Death Race 2000* (1975) would become one of the quintessential Corman movies, effortlessly mixing slapstick comedy, gross-out violence, acerbic humour, political commentary, gratuitous nudity and no small amount of hi-octane, four-wheeled mayhem.

With a budget of only $400,000, Corman had a lot less to work with than the upcoming film he was "inspired" by, but this wasn't his first rodeo. He couldn't afford any Hollywood stars, but he still found a lead actor who was a household name in his own right. Since 1972, David Carradine had been the star of *Kung Fu*, one of the biggest shows on television and a regular nominee/winner at the Primetime Emmy Awards. It was so successful, in fact, that by 1973 it had become the number one show on American TV, drawing a regular audience of 28 million viewers. Carradine was the face of *Kung Fu*, but his film career up until that point had been much more low-key,

with either decent parts in small productions or cameos in better-known movies such as *Mean Streets* (1973) and *The Long Goodbye* (1973). For *Death Race 2000*, he would be front and centre as Frankenstein, the greatest driver to ever play the game.

The rest of Corman's cast would be less familiar to contemporary audiences, but no less interesting for it. Former "Warhol Superstar" Mary Woronov had recently started forging an acting career away from 'The Factory', most recently in 1974's proto-slasher classic *Silent NIght, Bloody Night*, alongside Carradine's father John, while Martin Kove's future lay in imparting a "win at all costs" style of martial arts as the Cobra Kai sensei in *The Karate Kid* (1984). Most notably, an unknown actor by the name of Sylvester Stallone was cast as Machine Gun Joe Viterbo, Frankenstein's 1920s gangster-themed race rival. *Rocky* and global stardom were still a year away for young Sly, but he got probably the meatiest role out of anyone who doesn't ride in Frankenstein's alligator car and, if nothing else, he gives good meat...

After the world suffers a catastrophic global economic crash in 1979, civil unrest runs rife across America. A totalitarian government seizes control and places the country under martial law. By the year 2000, the population are pacified and under control, due in part to the distraction of the Transcontinental Road Race, a no-holds barred epic road race where pedestrians can be killed for added points.

Now in its 20th year, the undisputed king of the road is Frankenstein (David Carradine), so named as he has had many body parts repaired after a succession of near-fatal crashes. With his new navigator Annie Smith (Simone Griffeth) onboard, Frankenstein is pitted against four other drivers: the Nazi Matilda the Hun (Roberta Collins), the Roman gladiator-styled Nero the Hero (Martin Kove), the cowgirl Calamity Jane Kelly (Mary Woronov) and Machine Gun Joe Viterbo (Sylvester Stallone), who bases his look on vintage Chicago mobsters.

The opposition aren't the only threat though, as there is a resistance movement whose war against the Government involves setting deathtraps for the unsuspecting drivers along the route. Of course, there's also the Government themselves, who keep the whole country under their thumb with the Road Race and constant misinformation about a false war with those dastardly French. Frankenstein doesn't care about any of this though. His only focus is on winning yet another race. Or is it?

A cheaply made film that was rush-produced to cash in on the buzz before the release of a much bigger film really shouldn't be anything of any real worth, but Corman and director Paul Bartel really knock it out of the park with *Death Race 2000*. Sure, it's cheap, but it doesn't look *horribly* cheap. There are no misguided attempts to punch above their weight with effects or sets, so the lack of budget doesn't hobble it in any major ways.

That's not to say it doesn't have any ambition, as it builds an effective and vivid portrait of a world under the cosh of totalitarianism. A global crisis has been exploited by greed and lust for power by those in charge, and the population is kept under control by brute force, misinformation, targeted xenophobia and the distraction of entertainment. Crazy idea, eh?

In this grim future (21 years ago now), The President of the USA is a messianic figure, appearing on every television bathed in psychedelic lighting and blazing the French from his Summer Palace in, wait for it, Peking. When we finally see him in the flesh at the race's conclusion, he's much less impressive and psychedelic. Instead, he's a shabby little man whose power is clearly massively bolstered by smoke and mirrors. Standard politician, really. Like most dystopian futures, there's a class war at the heart of the conflict and *Death Race 2000* is no different. Here we have the downtrodden working class who are both the passive watchers of the race and the raw material for extra points that can be gained by running them over, but we also have a revolutionary movement that is standing up to the regime in any way they can. From our perspective, that means sabotaging the Transcontinental Road Race in a number of ways, from old-fashioned landmines to Road-Runner detours that go off cliffs to bombs disguised as babies. Yes, it's biting social commentary, but it doesn't take itself too seriously and that's a big part of why it works so well.

In fact, *Death Race 2000* is laugh-out-loud funny at times, while having some genuinely thrilling action sequences and extremely graphic violence in the mix, often all in the same sequence. Watching people being brutally run over isn't the most obvious source of comedy, especially when you see their heads going under the wheels, but Bartel balances it all perfectly. The violence is gratuitous, but so is the humour and the nudity. It's a sci-fi movie, for sure, but what it really is is a cartoon brought to life. If *Wacky Races* was remade by a gaggle of teenage boys, it would be *Death Race 2000*.

And what would *Wacky Races* be without a bunch of racers drawn in the broadest of strokes? Again, Corman and Bartel get it just right with their cast of four-wheeled maniacs. The limited budget means there are only five cars in this supposedly huge race, so *The Cannonball Run* it isn't, but what we get is more than enough. There's the brilliantly named Matilda the Hun who ticks the sexy evil Nazi box for maximum transgressive points; Nero

the Hero with his Roman leatherboy schtick; Woronov's all-American cowgirl Calamity Jane; and, to really drive home the *Wacky Races* influence, Stallone's Ant Hill Mob flesh golem Machine Gun Joe Viterbo. There's no major characterisation here other than they are all awful people, Joe in particular, but that's fine. It's a cartoon and they are there to be hissed at and meet an untimely end. Job done.

Then there's Frankenstein.

Initially, he's pitched as an awful person too. Clad in black leather and masked to hide his hideous facial injuries, he's an anti-hero, a jerk. He kills with no thought and is as cold as ice. As it turns out though, it's all an act. He's not scarred at all (the wonders of 1990s medicine) and even when he discovers his new co-pilot Annie is part of the resistance and plotting against him, he doesn't flinch. It looks like he's going to add her to his points total, but instead he brings her back in the car and into his confidence. He's not part of the resistance, but he's firmly on the same page and is planning to take out the President himself. How? Well, when he wins the race yet again (because he always wins), he's going to press the flesh with him and trigger a grenade he has implanted in his hand. Yes, it's a literal hand grenade! Far from being the mean-spirited killer he appears to be, Frankenstein is actually the hero this oppressed world needs and he's going to use the power he's been given by The Man to set things right.

He had many great roles, often in better movies than this, but Carradine really shines here and hits the complex beats of the character so well. Yes, he's a cold killer and even when we know he's on the side of the angels, he still goes out of his way to score points, but that just adds to his nihilistic charm and gives weight to how bad this regime is that a man like Frankenstein will still rise up. When we see his gentle and tender side, we realise he's far from a one-dimensional badass. For a knowingly dumb B-movie, it's not that dumb deep down.

The best thing about *Death Race 2000* isn't any of this, though. No, what really elevates it is its razor-sharp satire on the dark side of entertainment and the media. There's a Greek chorus of vapid, excitable idiots egging on the worst aspects of humanity here, playing their role in the dumbing down and oppression of their fellow man, spewing propaganda purporting to be news and information. It's a trope that's been well-used ever since in films like *Robocop* (1987), *Starship Troopers* (1997) and *Idiocracy* (2006) to name a few, and one that is still tragically relevant to this day, perhaps even more so. But in 1975, this was well ahead of the game.

Of course, *Death Race 2000* is trash and deliberately so, but it's also far, far smarter than it's letting on. Not bad for a cheap cash-in.

Three months after Corman had gazumped it, *Rollerball* made its appearance on the big screen and it hit like a spiked glove to the back of the head.

In the not-too distant future, the world is controlled by six global corporations: Energy, Food, Transport, Communications, Housing and Luxury. Nation states are a thing of the past, as is the concept of individuality. Society had been divided into a strict caste system: corporate executives at the top wielding absolute, unquestionable power; a middle class of the wealthy but powerless; and the working class who exist to serve and support. To help facilitate this, the Executive Committee has created Rollerball, a violent international sport that is designed to "demonstrate the futility of individual effort."

Veteran Houston team captain Jonathan E (Caan) has become the greatest Rollerball player in the history of the sport, leading and inspiring his team to victory again and again. This hasn't gone unnoticed by the Committee and, with the team only two games away from another triumphant season, Jonathan is told in no uncertain terms he is to retire from the sport he loves immediately. The captain resists and insists on playing with his team, leading the powers-that-be to take more drastic measures to deal with this growing threat to their authority. Penalties for violent conduct are eliminated, followed by substitutions meaning injured players can't leave the field of play, before even the idea of a time limit is done away with. If Jonathan E won't retire voluntarily, the last game of Rollerball will end when, at the bare minimum, one team is all dead...

Right from the off, you know exactly where you are with *Rollerball*. There are some big (if obvious) ideas about totalitarianism, freedom and the nature of man behind it all. But it's the game itself that the whole thing hangs on, and Jewison ensures that before we even get into any of that, Rollerball is firmly established as a real sport. The opening game is absolutely thrilling, a brutal, violent spectacle, but one with rules and tactics, every element of which is laid out in front of us. It's a lengthy sequence, but by its end, you know everything you need to know about this sport, and also a fair bit about the men who play it and the men who sit in the executive boxes calling the shots. We know all about the crowds too, the ones who all cheer on their team in identical clothing, a heaving, baying mass of collective identity that are being oppressed and don't even know it.

You know exactly who Jonathan E is too and Caan has much to do with that. The character's charisma is off the scale and he's utterly convincing as a man who could potentially wake up a world. He's tough and aggressive, but he's got no small amount of charm and an almost childlike joy in playing the game he loves, which makes his reaction to being told to quit all the more affecting. E is an apex predator on the ring, an alpha male of the highest order, but he's nothing compared to the true predators above him. They've already taken his wife from him and now the one thing he has left, that he loves more than anything... well, they're taking that too. Or so they think.

The world in which he lives is undoubtedly a grim dystopian future, but it's a comfortable one. Everyone is looked after to varying degrees, with hunger, poverty and war a thing of the past, but it comes at a price. Freedom is also a thing of the past, as is education and information. Libraries only contain edited summaries of books and even Zero, the central computer repository for information in Geneva, has lost the entire 13th Century and goes into conniptions when asked to explain how the world works. This is a society where nobody really knows who's calling the shots, but only one man is questioning it. It's no coincidence that Jonathan E wears the number 6 on his jersey. Because he's not a number, he's a free man. He just needed to be pushed too far to realise it.

Everyone else, from his doomed best pal and teammate Moonpie (John Beck) to his beloved former wife Ella (Maud Adams), just play the game and do what they are told without question. The corporations have set up a world where everyone is comfortable and distracted by easy living, feel-good drugs and and a constant stream of televised violence disguised as sport to channel any feelings of discontent or anger. Everyone is in the same boat and nothing ever changes. It's not designed to. Again, it's no coincidence that Rollerball is played on a loop and that final game has no way to leave or end. Rollerball is human society after the Corporate Wars in microcosm.

Interestingly, after that first visceral introduction to the game, it's about another hour before we see another one. Instead, the focus is very much on Jonathan's wakening, from a man who has grown to accept the status quo (even though it has cost him, making him close down emotionally unless he is on skates and smashing people). Crucially, we see that he isn't a thug or sadist, even choosing to put a new teammate in his place with humour when violence seems the most obvious response. Slowly, as his world threatens to collapse and his questions go unanswered, the individual the Executives fear so much comes to the fore. He's not just an individual though, he's a leader of men and they're right to fear him.

The big picture, as engaging as it is, pales in comparison with the actual game. The Rollerball action we see here is a high point of sports cinema, both in terms of drama and kinetic, edge-of-seat action. It is utterly, utterly riveting. You know the rules and you know at least some of the players, so by the time Houston plays Tokyo, you are firmly a Houston fan. Add in the tension of Jonathan playing on in defiance, the lack of penalties and the general upscaling of carnage, and you really have a game on your hands. There's much less joy in the faces of E and Moonpie this time around, as this isn't just another semi-final and they know it. The rules are being relaxed to either drive the captain out of the game or to kill him with no suspicion. And like what happens anytime man can act without fear of consequence, the results are grim. Moonpie gets his skull caved in by a group of Tokyo players and though his teammates get their revenge, a Rubicon has been crossed.

It all ends in the final against New York, the match with no rules and no end. Nobody even pretends to play Rollerball, they just kill each other until only Jonathan E and a single NY player is left. It's horrible to watch. As violent as the opening game in the film was, it's a far cry from the sport we see at the end. Brilliantly, with the crowd going full Roman Colosseum and baying for a killing

David Carradine in Death Race 2000

James Caan in Rollerball

blow, Jonathan E instead opts to spare his opponent and scores the only goal of the game. He's worked out just how many layers of a game he's been playing and realises truly for the first time why the Corporate Executives are so frightened of him and what he represents. It ends with him skating round the track, weaving in and out of fires, crashed motorbikes and the bodies of his teammates and rivals alike, with the entire crowd of both sets of fans chanting his name: "Jonathan... Jonathan... Jonathan!" He's not just a captain anymore, not just a legendary Rollerball player. He's a living legend and, although we don't see it, the smile on his face in that final freeze frame tells us all we need to know. The Executives were right to be afraid...

Unlike *Death Race 2000*, *Rollerball* takes itself oh-so seriously, but it hits the target every time. It offers a brutal vision of what was a near-future back in 1975 and isn't too far away from the world we live in right now. Sport has always been an obvious vehicle to comment on society, but in making his sport a fantastical science-fiction concept, Jewison paints a dark picture of where we could be headed if we don't pay attention.

The influence of *Rollerball* was seismic and continues to be felt to this day. Over in the UK, children's comics like 'Action' and '2000AD' slightly reworked the concept for strips like 'Death Game 1999' (1976-1979), 'Harlem Heroes' (1977) and 'Inferno' (1977-1978) much to the delight of children and dismay of parents, while Corman made an attempt to return to the well with 1978's *Deathsport*. Planned as a sequel to *Death Race 2000*, it would imaginatively feature motorbikes instead of cars and be set a thousand years in the future in a post-apocalyptic wasteland full of barbarian city states, mutant cannibals and lone warriors. It would also be an absolutely wretched affair that Corman struggled to get anyone to direct. He actively tried to dissuade star David Carradine from being involved in it. The actor would later insist that his career never really recovered from his participation in such a misstep.

Rollerball itself would be remade in 2002, starring *American Pie*'s Chris Klein and LL Cool J. Missing the entire point of Harrison and Jewison's story, John McTiernan bafflingly just opted to make a futuristic extreme sports film that was a box-office bomb and failed to even make back half its budget. Moving on...

Its legacy is more importantly realised in films such as *The Running Man* (1987), *Battle Royale* (2000) and *The Hunger Games* series (2012-2015). All of them might all have their genesis in works of literature, but deep in their DNA, there's an oppressed society being distracted by violent and deadly sports, waiting for a hero to stand up and lead them to freedom.

Doesn't sound all that different from the world we live in today, does it?

Altogether now: "Jonathan... Jonathan... Jonathan!"

Movie music connoisseur John Mansell examines a clutch of Wild West movies from the '70s, noting the way European westerns had a growing influence on American entries in the genre and vice versa. He also discusses the merits of the movie scores.

The Italian western - or 'spaghetti western' as it was nicknamed - made a great impression upon cinema. Genre entries were markedly differently in the wake of Leone's *Dollars* trilogy. The spaghettis were influenced by the Hollywood cowboy movies of yesteryear, notably the abundant B-pictures featuring the likes of Hopalong Cassidy and Roy Rogers. The Italians took key elements, themes and storylines from those pics and expanded upon them, creating antiheroes in place of clear good guys and bad guys. The formula was wildly successful, and it wasn't long before American filmmakers started copying it. From 1968 onwards, there was a definite sense that US filmmakers had come full circle and were now mimicking the European style of western which they themselves had once inspired. The inclusion of increased (some would say gratuitous) violence was particularly prominent.

This trend manifested itself as early as 1968 with Ted Post's spaghetti imitator *Hang 'em High* starring Clint Eastwood. There was also the Raquel Welch vehicle *100 Rifles* (1969) which co-starred Jim Brown and Burt Reynolds. As the '70s dawned, audiences began to realise just how influential Italian westerns had become, with Euro-flavoured movies like *Big Jake*, *Valdez is Coming*, *Five Savage Men (aka The Animals)*, *The McMasters*, *Soldier Blue*, *Barquero*, *El Condor*, etc. hitting cinema screens. A lot of that was due to the locations where they were shot. American filmmakers now forsook Arizona and Monument Valley, heading instead to Almeria in Spain to shoot their movies and often employing familiar faces from Italian productions such as Lee Van Cleef, and, of course, Clint Eastwood. According to many, the western (or, more specifically, the American western) was in decline, and this is probably why the Euro/Italian approach took off like it did. By combining the old-fashioned Hollywood way with the new style favoured by Leone, Corbucci, Sollima, et al, the money men in Tinseltown probably hoped the genre would enjoy a revival. And it worked, to a degree... though it wasn't long before stale old clichés and scenarios

began to creep back in, and the genre once again dipped in popularity.

Even Clint Eastwood's self-directed westerns contain strong elements of this Euro flavour. His first as director was *High Plains Drifter* (1973), in which he also starred. The score has a definite spaghetti influence, with the central theme by Dee Barton carrying an updated *The Grand Silence* vibe. Ennio Morricone had scored Sergio Corbucci's ultra-violent entry in 1968, and Barton's similar-sounding music comes across as mysterious yet strangely calming, lulling the audience into a false sense of security. Barton had previously scored *Play Misty for Me* (1971) for Eastwood, and the success of that collaboration meant Clint turned to him once more to fashion a suitable theme for *High Plains Drifter*. The film contains several other Italian influences - flashbacks; a stranger riding into town, playing both sides against the other for his own gain; the revenge element of the story. The actor-director would revisit similar themes on a larger scale for his near-remake *Pale Rider* in 1985. Barton's score plays a huge part within the framework of the movie, containing many nods to the music of the spaghetti western. There are atmospheric passages, racing timpani, electric guitar, a soprano voice (or at least a synthesised sound that resembles it), harmonica, whistle effects and tense, dramatic string strains that hiss their support to underline the mysterious vibe. The Morricone influence manifests itself predominantly in tracks such as *Dummy Wagon, Gunfight in Lago,* and *Dynamite*, with other cues such as *Bell Signal* evoking a rock-orientated sound similar to what composer Mario Migliardi gave us in *Matalo* (1970) or Stelvio Cipriani in *The Stranger Returns* (1967). The *High Plains Drifter* score was belatedly released by Intrada Records a few years ago.

(On a side note, it is somewhat surprising that *The Outlaw Josey Wales* (1976) is so removed stylistically from *High Plains Drifter*, with Eastwood returning to a more traditional Hollywood style. The violence is still there in abundance, and quirky comedic elements creep in to give a modicum of light relief, but the score by Jerry Fielding is more indebted to, say, Peckinpah than Leone, Corbucci and co.)

Heading back in time to 1970, *The McMasters* is a little-known offering directed by Swede Alf Kjellin. This tough entry has a sadistic streak and contains violence for the sake of it. It would possibly have been better if the makers had focused more on the important issues (e.g. racism after the American Civil War, or the question of whether the war was worth it when so many social/racial/class problems remained unresolved when the fighting ended). Despite an impressive cast which includes Burl Ives, Brock Peters, Jack Palance, David Carradine, John Carradine and Nancy Kwan, it falls short in a lot of areas. As alluded to already, it goes overboard from time to time with gratuitous moments such as a whipping and a rape.

Although filmed in and around Santa Fe, *The McMasters* was backed by a British company. As a result, it is a weird concoction of traditional western elements and Euro influences. It also has a rather bleak, defeatist tone. It's competent enough, but never really surprises you. It also doesn't deal thoroughly with the issues it raises. It is sometimes cited as a precursor to the spate of blaxploitation westerns which followed, like *The Legend of Nigger Charley*, *Buck and the Preacher* (both 1972), *Boss Nigger* and *Thomasine and Bushrod* (both 1974). Most of those upped the exploitation angle considerably. As for *The McMasters*, two versions were released - one approved by the producer, the other approved by the distributor. The full version has been scarcely seen over the years, but was made available on a recent French Blu-ray. Many of the easier-to-find versions have up to ten minutes excised, including the rape scene.

The music for *The McMasters* is the work of Afro-American composer Coleridge Taylor-Perkinson, who wrote predominantly for the concert hall and rarely ventured into TV or film work. He was born in 1932 in Manhattan, New York, and went on to become an innovative, inventive composer whose interests weren't confined to a single area of music. He often deviated and altered his style to accommodate concert hall symphonic compositions, jazz, dance and pop music. His score in *The McMasters*, though not particularly memorable, suits the movie and underlines the dramatic moments well. It elevates some of the action-led scenes, giving them greater power and adding a broader and more varied ambience.

Next for discussion is *Two Mules for Sister Sara* (1970), one of the earliest American-produced movies to take much of its style and appearance from the Italian format. Not only did it star Clint Eastwood (who had been the Man with No Name in Leone's *Dollars* trilogy), it also had a score by Morricone who had virtually invented the conventions of the spaghetti western sound. Don Siegel does his best to rekindle the spaghetti flavour in his directorial approach to the film. This is a good example of a Hollywood movie aping the stylisation of an Italian production. Ultimately, though, I can't help feeling it could have utilised these influences with more vigour and verve. Nevertheless, it's probably true to say that by the time Eastwood came to direct *High Plains Drifter*, he had learned a great deal from both Siegel and Leone, and combined both their styles to create his own unique brand of filmmaking.

Two Mules for Sister Sara was filmed in Mexico, which was a change from where many Hollywood westerns were shot. Normally, the prairies and the vast expanses of Monument Valley were used, but here the arid, heat-baked Mexican scrublands form the backdrop. It looks a lot like the dry and dusty Almeria countryside in Spain, where many Euro westerns were filmed. *Two Mules* has another Euro influence in that it has no hero but, rather, an anti-hero. Hogan (Eastwood) looks out for no-one but himself most of the time, at least until he meets Sister Sara (Shirley MacLaine)... but even *she* is not what the audience expects her to be.

It's a good movie, admittedly not on the same level as the *Dollars* films but certainly interesting and eventful. Morricone's score is one of his best in the genre, enlisting the sound of a braying mule in the central theme and combining it with a nuns' chorus which is both angelic and somewhat irreverent. Compared with the score for *The Good, The Bad, and The Ugly*, the *Two Mules for Sister Sara* score is quite sparse, with instrumentation that is rarely grandiose. A cue called *The Battle* is the exception, a highly dramatic piece which seems out of place against the rest of the soundtrack. It evokes Morricone's pulsating, jagged march from *The Battle of Algiers*. As with every Morricone score, *Two Mules* is wonderfully quirky. The movie is well liked by Eastwood fans and western connoisseurs, and the music is undoubtedly a big factor in its popularity.

Five Savage Men (1970) aka *The Animals* was released the same year as *Two Mules for Sister Sara,* but lacks its presence and inventiveness. To be honest, this is another example of an American movie which apes the Italian influence in a less than good way. It's a revenge western, with a band of brigands robbing a stagecoach and killing everyone on board apart from a young teacher. They abduct her, take her to their hideout and use her for their pleasure until she is dead… or so they think. They leave her and ride off to do more unspeakable things, but she is found and saved by an Apache chief who nurses her back to health. After realising what she has gone through, the chief shows her how she can take revenge on her brutal attackers. (A similar theme is also explored in *Hannie Caulder* (1971) and crops up again two years later in the 1973 western *A Man Called Noon*, which had an English director but was actually an Italian/Spanish co-production).

Five Savage Men is not particularly well made. In fact, it is one of the most unworthy additions to the genre from the '70s. But at this time, American filmmakers were desperate to emulate or imitate the themes and violent scenarios that European filmmakers depicted so often, in the hope of garnering a successful formula. The film does at least boast a well-known cast, including Henry Silva, Keenan Wynn and Michelle Carey as the female lead. By the end, you almost feel sorry for the bad guys, because the victim becomes such an unmerciful murderer, a lethal avenging angel figure, that her revenge on the outlaws is pretty sadistic. Each time she dispatches one of the gang members, we are given a flashback to her torturous ordeal to remind us that they deserve their fate.

The music is credited to Rupert Holmes, a successful vocalist and songwriter (he actually performs the song heard over the closing credits). He is listed as the composer too, but I'm not certain this is correct (there are no other feature film credits on his resumé). It's likely he *was* involved, but his themes were probably arranged and orchestrated by an uncredited composer or conductor, probably someone with more experience scoring movies. Like *The McMasters*, *Five Savage Men* could have been better if the director had toned down the violence just a little (though I do concede some violence was necessary within the context of the storyline). A soundtrack album was never released, which is a shame because it deserves to be heard (in fact, the score is considerably better than the film itself!)

To 1972 next, and *The Revengers*. This ultra-violent movie reunites William Holden and Ernest Borgnine in a bid to rekindle the magic of *The Wild Bunch*. The scenes where Holden's family are found after being massacred were heavily censored or removed completely for television showings. It is a good movie though, entertaining on many levels, and I personally rank it among my top twenty westerns despite the critical panning it endured at the time. Directed by Daniel Mann and produced by Martin Rackin, it is (as its title indicates) a tale of revenge with Holden gathering a Dirty Dozen-type troupe of ex-cons and murderers to track down the killers who wiped out his family.

There are many Italian-influenced trademarks in the film, mostly violent and quirky interludes which the director cleverly combines with more established and familiar tropes from Hollywood westerns like *The Magnificent*

Seven and *The Searchers.*

The Revengers contains a somewhat colourful musical score by composer/pianist Pino Calvi. His upbeat music is evocative of earlier scores by composers like Piero Piccioni and Gianni Ferrio. The soundtrack was issued on an LP at the time of release but was soon deleted. There was a later CD release on the Screen Trax label, but the tracks were taken from the original vinyl LP recording and one can, at times, hear a few pops and scratches. It is undoubtedly a score that deserves being remastered and reissued. Calvi's music is fast-paced and exhilarating, combining elements of the spaghetti sound and more traditional American western flourishes. Calvi generates a jazz-oriented persona and a distinct spaghetti flavour at the same time. He achieves a wonderful balance - dramatic and melancholy, vibrant and robust - especially during the set pieces. It is believed the original master tapes were lost or destroyed (many masters were thrown out by studios in the '70s, as they didn't foresee any future use for them), and this is a crying shame.

Of course, there were a few Italian/American co-productions such as *Take a Hard Ride* (1975) in which the audience was treated to the best of both worlds. What I mean by that is that American and Italian western conventions were mixed almost equally. The film stars Jim Brown and Lee Van Cleef, reunited after working together in *El Condor* (another American western that was influenced by the spaghetti style). Van Cleef appeared in a lot of these pics - *Barquero, Captain Apache, Kid Vengeance, The Magnificent Seven Ride, Return of Sabata, etc.* His pairing with Jim Brown in *Take a Hard Ride* really pays off, as the movie is an entertaining romp which proved deservedly popular at the box office. It is directed by Antonio Margheriti (who often went under the alias Anthony M. Dawson). The director had worked on the special effects for Sergio Leone's *A Fistful of Dynamite* and made a handful of serviceable Italian westerns such as *And God Said to Cain* (1970). His most prominent spaghetti oater, however, was *Vengeance* (1968). The director also helmed several horror movies and sword-and-sandal adventures.

Take a Hard Ride is scored by the legendary Jerry Goldsmith, who pays homage to the Italian western score at key points by adding little trills and nuances that identify with certain characters. Ennio Morricone had done similar musical leitmotifs in *A Fistful of Dollars* and *Once Upon a Time in the West.* The film is certainly shaped in the Italian mould, but it also contains many stock qualities associated with Hollywood westerns.

As the '70s progressed, it's hard to say exactly which American westerns were influencing the Italian ones, and which Italian ones were influencing the American ones. The aping, mimicking, borrowing and ripping-off became almost interchangeable. Nevertheless, it was an interesting period for the genre, with fascinating movies being made and memorable scores being composed throughout.

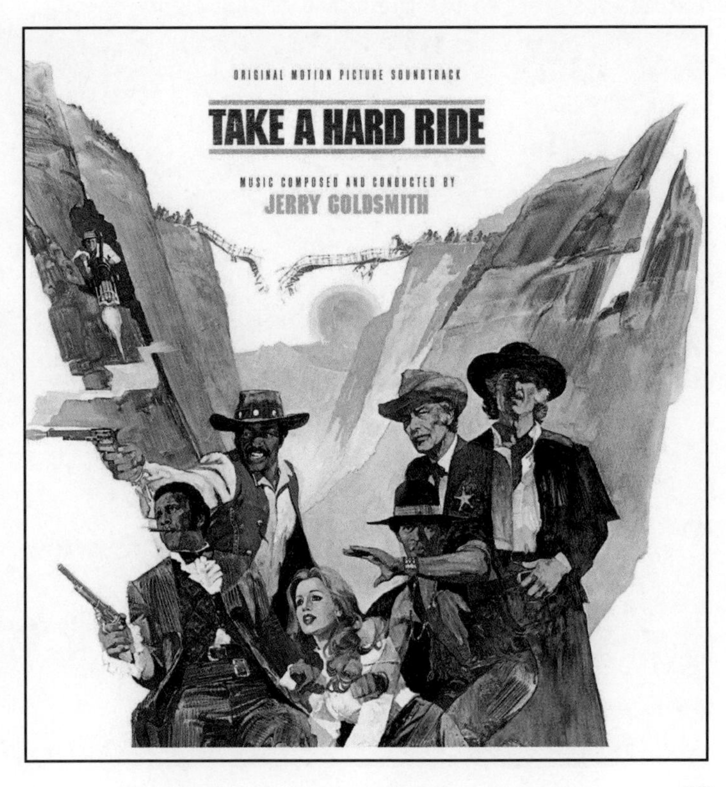

PHANTOM of the PARADISE

by Dawn Dabell

If you mention director Brian De Palma, most people will associate him with horror, crime and Hitchcockian psychological thrillers. *Sisters (1972), Obsession (1976), Carrie (1976), The Fury (1978), Dressed to Kill (1980), Blow Out (1981), Scarface (1983), Body Double (1984)* and *The Untouchables (1987)* are generally the first titles which spring to mind. It's difficult to visualise a rock musical fitting into such an oeuvre, but amongst these better-known offerings De Palma did in fact direct and write that very thing - *Phantom of the Paradise* (1974).

Released a year before *The Rocky Horror Picture Show*, De Palma's film was to be relatively overshadowed by Richard O'Brien's much-loved, quirky musical. *Rocky Horror* seemed to get bigger and bigger as the years went by, especially with the introduction of regular singalong screenings during which fans donned their favourite character's costumes. *Phantom* was more of a sleeper, and it took years for it to build up its status as a cult classic. In the recent past, a DVD version won a richly deserved Rondo Hatton Classic Horror Award for Best Extras - it's great to see the movie getting plenty of long overdue recognition of that type. Unlike *Rocky Horror* (and countless others from the genre), the musical numbers do not show cast members breaking out in song at random moments. Instead, the singing is kept in context with the characters either singing during a rehearsal or on stage as part of a musical act. It wouldn't necessarily have been a bad thing if some of the characters expressed their feelings towards each other through song and dance, but it doesn't hinder things either by not having them behave in such a way.

The influences on the plot are drawn from far and wide, almost overwhelmingly so. One might describe it as a mash-up of Gaston Leroux's *The Phantom of the Opera*, Oscar Wilde's *The Picture of Dorian Gray* and Johann Wolfgang von Goethe/Christopher Marlowe's *Faust*, with numerous other classical narratives thrownin for good measure. De Palma was often heavily influenced by others; many of his films are variations on something which existed already, told from his own uniquely offbeat perspective. And as such, *Phantom of the Paradise* is, like so many of De Palma's movies, a highly worthwhile viewing experience.

Naive composer Winslow Leach (Willian Finley) has his musical cantata stolen by the infamous music impresario Swan (Paul Williams). While trying to reclaim his prized composition, Winslow is beaten by Swan's lackeys. He's framed for drug offences and sent to prison. Winslow escapes from jail, but while attempting to break into Swan's place he burns his face on a record pressing machine. He is forced to wear a mask to hide his now-deformed appearance, and takes on the persona of 'The Phantom', swearing his revenge on the evil, pint-sized Swan.

It also transpires there is more to the youthful-looking Swan than first meets the eye… he has, in fact, sold his soul for eternal youth and now himself deals in the buying of other people's souls. Swan intends to open a rock palace, the Paradise, with Winslow's musical cantata being the main attraction. Winslow, who has fallen in love with a free-spirited singer named Phoenix (Jessica Harper), wishes for her to perform his music during the grand opening of this new venue. He will stop at nothing to ensure this happens. But Swan has other ideas, and intends to let male singer Beef (Gerrit Graham) take the lead. This leads to to the Phantom wreaking havoc on the Paradise and anyone who gets in his way!

De Palma often tried to pay homage to Alfred Hitchcock in his films. He described Hitch as "… the one who distilled the essence of film. He's like Webster. It's all there. I've used a lot of his grammar." Over the years, many of De Palma's films featured scenes undoubtedly influenced by Hitchcock, *Body Double* and *Dressed to Kill* being obvious examples. *Phantom of the Paradise* is far removed from anything Hitchcock worked on, but De Palma still manages to work in occasional tributes, such as a brilliant *Psycho*-inspired shower scene. The sequence is played for laughs, with the Phantom sneaking up on Beef while he showers, attacking him with a plunger rather than stabbing him in cold blood. The Phantom merely wants to warn him to leave the singing to Phoenix. If only Beef had heeded this advice...

Lead actor Finley met De Palma while studying at Columbia University and they became lifelong friends. Throughout his acting career, Finley appeared in nine of the director's films, starting with the student short *Woton's Wake* (1963) (the actor's debut). *Murder a la Mod* (1968), *The Wedding Party* (1969), *Sisters* (1972), *Phantom of the Paradise* (1974), *Obsession* (1976), *The Fury* (1978), *Dressed to Kill* (1980) and *The Black Dalia* (2006) followed. His role(s) in *Phantom of the*

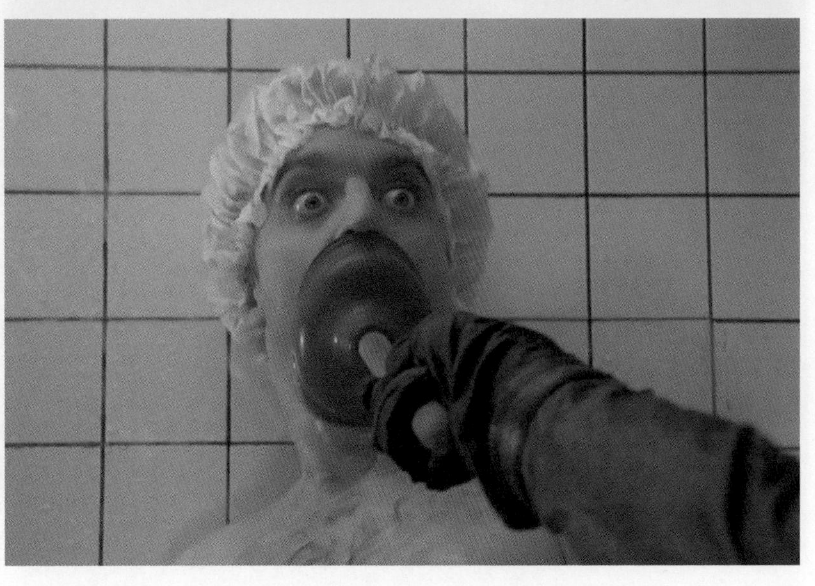

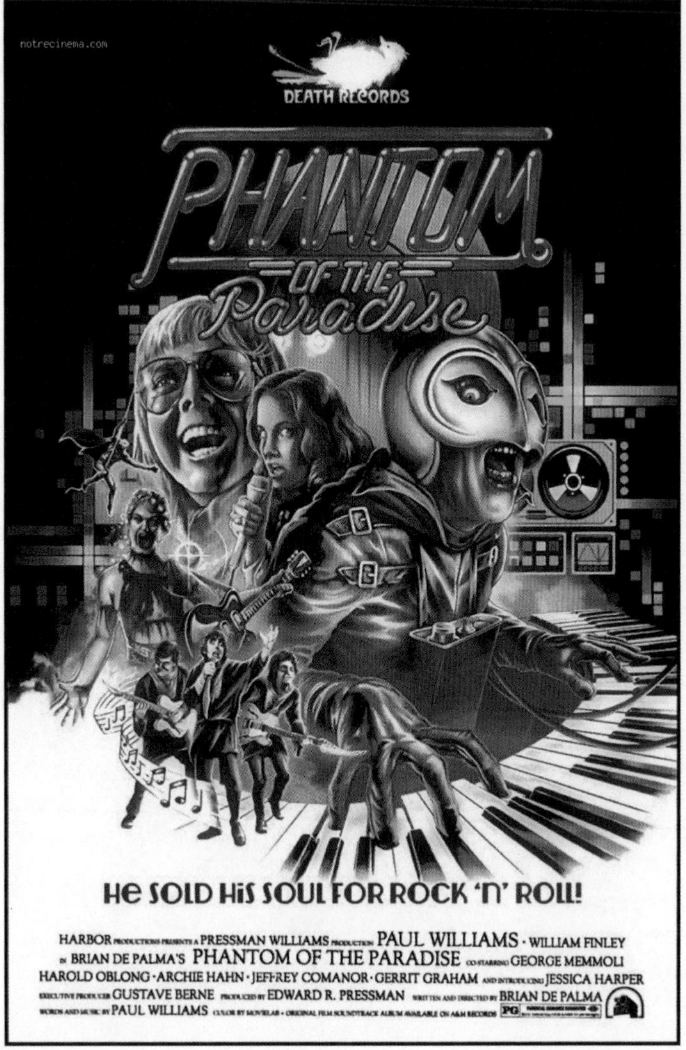

Paradise proved to be his most notorious and iconic, with an ever-growing cult fan base championing it over more recent years.

Although the role of Winslow was originally written with Finley in mind, there were some concerns regarding his bankability as the lead. The idea of casting Williams in the role was bandied about, with Gerrit Graham (Beef) playing the evil producer Swan and Peter Boyle playing Beef. In the end, Boyle turned down the part, and Finley landed the Phantom role as De Palma had originally intended. I'm sure most viewers will agree the right actors got the right parts in the end. Everyone seems perfectly in tune with their character. It's particularly difficult to imagine anyone but Finley as Winslow/the Phantom. The actor doesn't have traditional leading actor looks, but he's perfect as the put-upon underdog who tries to stand up to Swan to reclaim his music.

Jessica Harper - generally associated with her role in Dario Argento's supernatural giallo *Suspiria* (1977) - makes her big-screen debut as Phoenix, a talented singer with whom Winslow has fallen head-over-heels in love. As well as acting, Harper was also adept at singing, having performed in the Broadway musical *Hair*. She auditioned for the part of Phoenix against American singer Linda Ronstadt and ended up landing the role. Winning the role came as a surprise to Harper. In an interview, she stated: "I don't know why she [Linda] didn't get the part but it certainly was not because she was lacking in any way." Whatever the reason behind the casting of Harper, she is the perfect choice. As the free-spirited singer, she is simply captivating. People may be curious to learn that Harper would go on to play the role of Janet Majors (née Weiss) in *Shock Treatment* (1981), the sequel to *The Rocky Horror Picture Show*. It's an intriguing connection in view of how often *Phantom* and *Rocky Horror* are compared to each other.

After being considered for the Winslow role, Paul Williams didn't feel he was right for the character and feared he wouldn't be imposing enough. Thankfully, when the actors were shuffled around, he ended up perfectly cast as the unscrupulous, baby-faced music mogul swan. Williams was a bit of a 'jack-of-all-trades' - not only was he a capable actor, he was also a singer, songwriter and composer. These skills proved invaluable here. Besides playing Swan, he also provided the soundtrack and featured on the vocals for a number of the songs. *Phantom* garnered a lot of negative reviews at the time of release, but was praised for its music. Williams' soundtrack was nominated for a number of awards, including an Acadamy Award for Best Music and a Golden Globe for Best Original Score. It may have initially been a box-office flop but the brilliance of the music was acknowledged right from the start. Throughout the '70s, Williams was involved with other well-known features, penning songs for *A Star is Born*

(1976) *Bugsy Malone* (1976) and *The Muppets Movie* (1979) to name a few. The high point was the love ballad *Evergreen* from *A Star Is Born* which won him an Academy Award for Best Original Song and a Grammy for Song of the Year.

Gerrit Graham deserves a special mention as the over-the-top rock-and-roll singer Beef. Explaining how De Palma envisioned his character, Graham explained: "He flew me out from New York to meet with Paul Williams and the two of them kept making this Beef character seem more like Little Richard. 'What do you want?' I said. They said: 'flamboyant!', which, at the time in Hollywood, meant gay! So, I did a few lines in the Beef accent and lisp and they loved it. They burst into laughter and said: 'that's it!' That's how the character was born." There's no denying that Gerrit is impressive in every scene, whether wearing rollers in his hair, performing on stage in his glittery outfits or even wearing a feminine shower cap during one of the funniest moments. He really carries it off, almost stealing the show from the others.

Having received high praise for her standout performance in *Badlands* (1973), it's rather surprising to find future Oscar-winner Sissy Spacek credited as the set dresser on De Palma's film. She'd met her soon-to-be-husband John Frisk on the set of *Badlands,* and when Fisk was hired as Production Designer on *Phantom of the Paradise*, he brought her along to work with him. This may seem on the surface a strange transgression for the actress, but in a sense it led to her auditioning for the role of Carrie White in *Carrie*. You see, Frisk was hired by De Palma for the Stephen King adaptation and encouraged his wife to try for the lead part. Since *Carrie* is considered by many to be De Palma's greatest film, it's fair to say everything panned out perfectly! Fisk, Spacek and the rest of the behind-the-scenes team make a great contribution in making *Phantom of the Paradise* so visually appealing and striking.

Prior to release, the production ran into a number of legal difficulties. The one which proved the most problematic was the inclusion of 'Swan Song Enterprises' within the narrative. Peter Grant (Led Zeppelin's manager) had created an actual company called Swan Song Records and, as a result of this, Grant threatened to stop *Phantom of the Paradise* from being released. De Palma and his editor, Paul Hirsch, were forced to remove any prominent references to 'Swan Song' in post-production, painstakingly going through and re-cutting scenes (and changing the name of Swan's company to Death Records) by hand. Implementing these edits racked up an estimated $22,000 of additional costs. Every so often, viewers may still spot references to 'Swan Song' on signs or in the background, but enough of the references were masked to avoid a lawsuit.

Contemporary critic Pauline Kael was fairly positive in her assessment of *Phantom of the Paradise*. She wrote, in 'The New Yorker' (November 11, 1974): "De Palma is drawn to rabid visual exaggeration and sophisticated, satirical low comedy. This slapstick expressionism is idiosyncratic in the extreme. It's De Palma's flukiness that makes *Phantom* so entertaining."

Phantom of the Paradise is fabulously entertaining. Although I'm a devout *Rocky Horror* fan, this rock musical is a very worthy rival. If you haven't seen it, be sure to rectify that ASAP!

A portrait of Winslow Leach, the Phantom, by Paul Garner (above).

YOU CAN'T WIN 'EM ALL

by Jonathon Dabell

You Can't Win 'em All (1970) was originally going to be called *The Dubious Patriots*. Burt Kennedy was announced as director early on but took a hike before shooting commenced. Several sources suggest Howard Hawks was attached to the project too. In the end, it fell to British filmmaker Peter Collinson to take the reins, hot off the success of his best (and most popular) pic *The Italian Job* (1969).

Collinson had a reputation for being something of a tyrant. He was very strict and opinionated, and was known to be punishingly tough on his actors. Susan George, who worked with him on the babysitter-in-peril thriller *Fright* (1971), later recalled that he was extremely forthright and demanding. During the shooting of his final film, *The Earthling* (1980), he repeatedly reduced child actor Ricky Schroder to tears, forcing star William Holden to step in to stick up for the kid.

Shooting on *You Can't Win 'em All* took place in Turkey between July and October 1969. Despite the colourful, exotic locations, it was a somewhat unhappy shoot. Charles Bronson was in no mood to be bullied and harried by the tough-talking director, and this resulted in an atmosphere of considerable tension between them. When the film underperformed at the box office and left critics underwhelmed, Collinson was quick to blame Bronson. He accused the actor of working against him throughout the entire filming process. Tony Curtis felt Collinson was at fault, both for the film's weaknesses and the miserable conditions they'd been forced to endure on set. "The thing that did us in was the very shoddy British production set up," the actor said. "They promised certain things on location and didn't provide them. There were inadequate sanitary conditions: people got sick. The director Peter Collinson? I have no comment about Mr. Collinson. Someday I'll tell you about him!"

The script was by Leo V. Gordon, better known as a solid character actor from the likes of *Riot in Cell Block 11* (1954), *The Haunted Palace* (1963) and *McLintock!* (1963). He dropped the 'V' (which stood for Vincent) from his name when acting and preferred to be credited just as Leo Gordon. But when he had his writing hat on (which was often, as he scripted prolifically over the years), he included the 'V' in his name. Gordon reserves a good role for himself in *You Can't Win 'em All* as one of Bronson's grizzled mercenaries.

The historical backdrop against which Gordon sets his screenplay is quite fascinating. It deals with a period of history rarely covered in cinema. The Greco-Turkish War was fought in the aftermath of WW1 (from May 1919 to October 1922 to be precise) and stemmed from the complex post-war situation in an area previously known as the Ottoman Empire. The region was being partitioned now The Great War was over. Various countries were involved in volatile negotiations and the drawing up of new borders. Almost inevitably, fighting broke out and three years of further violence and destruction left thousands dead and many towns and cities obliterated. It's doubtful many viewers in 1970 (or after) would have known much about the different sides of the battle, the shifting allegiances, who sympathised with who, and what exactly they were fighting for. This results in moments where it's difficult to tell who is being attacked by whom, or why. Gordon's script doesn't make the situation particularly clear, opting to concentrate on carnage and action (with occasional comedy). It's all very noisy, chaotic and action-packed (with one of the highest body-counts I can recall outside of a *Rambo* pic), but the finer details of the Greco-Turkish War backdrop are barely explained.

Against the fighting, we are introduced to two soldiers of fortune who are brought together by chance. (I use 'together' loosely, as at different points in the story they go from saving each other's lives to double-crossing each other for financial gain, always with a smile on their face and a twinkle in their eye). Adam Dyer (Curtis) owned a small fleet of three ships during the Great War, but two of them were destroyed and his brother and father went down with them. He believes the third is now in Turkish hands and wants to claim it back. "I lost everything in the Big War; maybe I can get some of it back in a small one," he remarks. Josh Corey (Bronson) is simply looking for his next big payday. A tough, taciturn mercenary, he will work for any side and take on any job as long as the money is right.

They end up agreeing to escort the daughters of Osman Bey (Grégoire Aslan), an Ottoman governor, to Smyrna. It is a dangerous journey, fraught with risk, and the perils escalate exponentially when they learn a gold shipment will be transported with the girls at the same time. There is another woman in the party, the mysterious Aila (Michèle Mercier), who seems to be carrying something even more valuable than gold.

When Adam discovers the gold is really lead, painted over to appear more precious, his suspicions are roused. An accompanying soldier, Colonel Elci (Fikret Hakan, dubbed in the English version by the instantly recognisable Robert Rietti), seems to be in cahoots with Aila. It looks like the two of them have plans to make off with whatever she is carrying. But Adam and Josh have eyes for Aila too, and are keen to get their hands on her mysterious cargo (and maybe, if they're lucky, the woman herself). The result is lots of conspiring, one-upmanship, deceiving and double-crossing.

It's surprising that Curtis was top billed over Bronson here. He'd been a big movie star from the mid '50s but his

clout was waning by the time this film was made (the TV show *The Persuaders* would reinvent him as a charismatic TV actor, but his heyday on the big screen was over). Bronson still hadn't cracked America but was huge in Europe. Three of his recent films - *Farewell, Friend* (1968), *Once Upon a Time in the West* (1968) and *Rider on the Rain* (1970) - had smashed box office records in countries like France.

Regardless of the miserable conditions and uneasy relationship with their director, Curtis and Bronson show undeniable chemistry and bounce off each other well. Curtis' character has a sort of cheeky charm comparable to Cary Grant. We never believe he is in danger for a moment; his apparent immunity to the thousands of bullets being fired works against plausibility and excitement. But he is immensely likable and brings a lot of fun to the pic. Bronson looks particularly ripped and formidable. He does the tough stuff well, machine-gunning his way across the country with glee.

One of the main theatrical posters by Frank McCarthy shows Curtis, Bronson and Mercier armed to the teeth straddling the front of a train, with explosions and other action pictured in the background. It's perhaps my favourite movie poster of all time, promising non-stop thrills and action. The film doesn't live up to this poster, of course (how could it?) but still has plenty of big bangs, violence, treachery and adventure. Alas, the muddled script and unclear contextual background make it hard to engage with the action. While it looks absolutely great on a visual level, the noise and mayhem alone aren't quite enough. Spectacle is fine, but it needs to be backed up with heart. We, the viewers, need to be fully absorbed in the story if we're going to get emotionally involved. And most of the time, we aren't.

Nevertheless, *You Can't Win 'em All* is constantly busy and handsomely shot: Ken Higgins' cinematography makes the dusty Turkish locales look beautiful to the eye, and Bert Kaempfert provides a thunderous score which complements the action. Yes, it has weaknesses and yes, it's hard to follow, but there's enough here to warrant a look. And who wouldn't want that gorgeous McCarthy poster framed on their wall?!?

Caricatures by Aaron Stielstra

Timothy Carey in *The Outfit* (1973)
(pg.59)

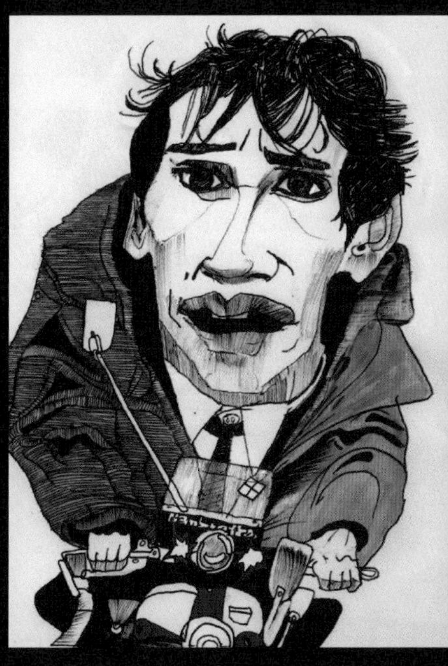

Phil Daniels in *Quadrophenia* (1979)
(pg. 38)

Robert Ryan in *The Outfit* (1973)
(pg.59)

Hal Ashby and Jack Nicholson
(pg.24)

CLOSING CREDITS

Rachel Bellwoar
Rachel is a writer for 'Comicon', 'Diabolique' magazine and 'Flickering Myth'. If she could have any director fim a biopic about her life it would be Aki Kaurismäki.

Jules Boyle
Jules is a music and film journalist from Glasgow. As lead music writer for the 'Sunday Mail' newspaper's 'Seven Nights' magazine, he has interviewed everyone from John Carpenter and David Duchovny to Public Enemy, U2 and Chic. A horror obsessive since the age of three according to his understanding parents, he scratches that itch with his 31 Days series of film reviews on the Big Comic Page website, as well as regular contributions to 'We Belong Dead' magazine. His first book, a comprehensive look at the classic era of British horror, will be released at the end of 2021.

David Michael Brown
David is a British ex-pat living in Sydney. Working as a freelance writer he has contributed to 'The Big Issue', 'TV Week', 'GQ', 'Rolling Stone' and 'Empire Magazine Australia', where he was Senior Editor for almost eight years. He is presently writing a book on the film music of German electronic music pioneers Tangerine Dream and researching the work of Andy Warhol associate and indie filmmaker Paul Morrissey for a forthcoming project.

Dawn Dabell
Dawn runs her own clothing business in West Yorkshire. When she's not busy selling fabulous dresses and quirky tops, she's a full-time film enthusiast, writer and mum! She has written for 'Cinema Retro', 'We Belong Dead', 'Monster!' and 'Weng's Chop', and is also the co-author of 'More Than a Psycho: The Complete Films of Anthony Perkins' (2018) and 'Ultimate Warrior: The Complete Films of Yul Brynner' (2019). She is also the co-creator and designer of the very mag you're holding in your hands right now.

Jonathon Dabell
Jonathon was born in Nottingham in 1976. He is a huge film fan and considers '70s cinema his favourite decade. He has written for 'Cinema Retro' and 'We Belong Dead', and co-authored 'More Than a Psycho: The Complete Films of Anthony Perkins' and 'Ultimate Warrior: The Complete Films of Yul Brynner' with his wife. He lives in Yorkshire with his wife, three kids, three cats and two rabbits!

Martin Dallard
Fed on a staple diet of *The Six Million Dollar Man*, the Adam West *Batman* show and the likes of *The Flashing Blade* and *Champion the Wonder Horse* from a young age, it's no wonder Martin is a self-confessed geek for all things '70s. Don't get him started on the likes of Ron Ely's *Doc Savage,* as you'll never hear the end of it! Whether it travelled in a TARDIS, or it rode in a red double decker bus, he watched it!

Andy Ellis
Andy (a.k.a. Location Finder General) is a huge film fan, lover of all genres (especially horror), who has become addicted in the last decade to photographing film locations.

David Flack
David was born and bred in Cambridge. Relatively new to the writing game, he has had reviews published in 'We Belong Dead' and 'Cinema of the '70s'. He loves watching, talking, reading and writing about film and participating on film forums. The best film he has seen in over 55 years of watching is *Jaws* (1975). The worst is *The Creeping Terror* (1963) or anything by Andy Milligan.

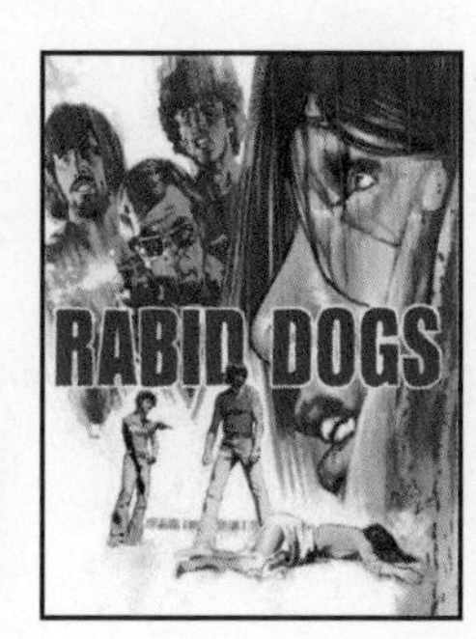

John H. Foote

John is a critic/film historian with thirty years experience. He has been a film critic on TV, radio, print criticism, newspaper and the web, for various sites including his own, Foote and friends on film.com. He spent ten years as Director of the Toronto Film School, where he taught Film History, and has written two books. The first was an exploration of the films directed by Clint Eastwood, the second a massive volume of the works of Steven Spielberg. Scorsese is next. John has interviewed everyone in film, except Jack Nicholson he quips. His obsession with film began at age 13.

John Harrison

John is a Melbourne, Australia-based freelance writer and film historian who has written for numerous genre publications, including 'Fatal Visions', 'Cult Movies', 'Is It Uncut?', 'Monster!' and 'Weng's Chop'. Harrison is also the author of the Headpress book 'Hip Pocket Sleaze: The Lurid World of Vintage Adult Paperbacks', has recorded audio commentaries for Kino Lorber, and composed the booklet essays for the Australian Blu-ray releases of *Thirst, Dead Kids* and *The Survivor*. 'Wildcat!', Harrison's book on the film and television career of former child evangelist Marjoe Gortner, was published by Bear Manor in 2020.

Julian Hobbs

Julian's lifelong love of scary movies began when he was 5 or 6, after being severely traumatized by a TV screening of George Pal's *War of the Worlds*. Several decades later later, Mark Berry asked him to contribute some DVD reviews to his 'Naked' magazine (no, not that kind of mag...) and the film writing bug caught him. He has written for 'We Belong Dead' and its various book offshoots. If he wasn't writing, he'd be beating the skins quite loudly in various Bristol bands. Julian is currently employed within the private health sector after a stint supporting the NHS.

Darren Linder

Darren grew up in the '70s and has been forever enamored with films from that decade. He is a lifelong resident of Oregon, currently living in Portland. He has performed in many rock bands, ran a non-profit dog rescue, and worked in social service with at-risk youth. Currently he works security in music venues, and is completing a book about his experiences there to be published later this year. His favorite film directors of the '70s are Sam Peckinpah, Francis Ford Coppola and William Friedkin.

John Mansell

John is a film music collector at heart, his passion for film music is something that has been with him since 1962. A member of the International film music critics association, he runs and edits 'Movie Music International'' and has interviewed over 120 film music composers and written notes for over 100 CD releases all of which are soundtracks. He has contributed to 'Variety' magazine and provided the entire film music section for the 'Variety International' film guide in 1996. He is currently writing a book on film music and composers.

Eric McNaughton

Eric invented the first ever time machine in 1889 and travelled to the 21st century where he is now stuck editing books and magazines on the classic world of horror.

Brian J. Robb

Brian is the 'New Yoirk Times' and 'Sunday Times' bestselling biographer of Leonardo Di Caprio, Keanu Reeves, Johnny Depp and Brad Pitt. He has also written books on silent cinema, the films of Philip K. Dick, horror director Wes Craven, and classic comedy team Laurel and Hardy, the *Star Wars* movies, Superheroes, Gangsters, and Walt Disney, as well as science fiction television series *Doctor Who* and *Star Trek*. His illustrated books include a History of Steampunk and an award-winning guide to J.R.R. Tolkien's Middle-earth. A former magazine and newspaper editor, he was co-founder of the Sci-Fi bulletin website and lives near Edinburgh.

Joseph Secrett

Joseph is a film nut and collector who started at a young age, and quickly became infatuated with all things cinematic. He is a huge fan of 20th century cinema, especially the '60s and '70s for their sheer diversity of genres. Top choices of his include revisionist westerns and seedy crime dramas.

Ian Taylor

Ian dabbled in horror fiction in the early '90s before writing and editing music fanzines. He later adjudicated plays for the Greater Manchester Drama Federation but enjoys film analysis most. Over the last five years, he has become a regular writer and editorial team member for 'We Belong Dead' magazine and contributed to all their book releases. This has led to writing for Dez Skinn's 'Halls of Horror', Allan Bryce's 'Dark Side' and Hemlock's 'Fantastic Fifties', amongst others. His first solo book 'All Sorts of Things Might Happen: The Films of Jenny Agutter' was recently released as a 'We Belong Dead' publication.

Printed in Great Britain
by Amazon